CHRISTIE'S
Century of
TEDDY BEARS

LEYLA MANIERA

CHRISTIE'S
Century of
TEDDY BEARS

LEYLA MANIERA

PAVILION

FOR WILLIAM

First published in 2001 in Great Britain by
PAVILION BOOKS LIMITED

An imprint of **Chrysalis** Books Group plc

The Chrysalis Building, Bramley Road
London, W10 6SP

This paperback edition first published
in 2003 by Pavilion Books Limited

DESIGNED BY: Balley Design Associates

A CIP catalogue record for this book is available
from the British Library

ISBN 1 86205 5955

Set in Bembo
Printed in Portugal by Printer Portuguese

1 2 3 4 5 6 7 8 9 10

This book can be ordered direct from the publisher.
Please contact the Marketing Department.
But try your bookshop first.

contents

ABOUT CHRISTIE'S

The name of Christie's is identified throughout the world with art, expertise and connoisseurship.

In 1766 James Christie opened his London auction house and launched the world's first fine art auctioneers. Christie's reputation was established in its early years, when James Christie's saleroom became a fashionable gathering place for Georgian society, as well as for knowledgeable collectors and dealers. Christie offered artists the use of his auction house to exhibit their works and enjoyed the friendship of leading figures of the day such as Sir Joshua Reynolds, Thomas Chippendale and Thomas Gainsborough. Christie's conducted the greatest auctions of the eighteenth and nineteenth centuries, selling works of art that now hang in the world's great museums.

Over its long history, Christie's has grown into the world's leading auction house, offering sales in over eighty separate categories which include all areas of the fine and decorative arts, collectables, wine, stamps, motor cars, even sunken cargo. There are hundreds of auctions throughout the year selling objects of every description and catering to collectors of every level.

Buyers and browsers alike will find that Christie's galleries offer changing exhibitions to rival any museum. Unlike most museums, however, in the salerooms you can touch each object and examine it up close.

Auctions are an exciting way to buy rare and wonderful objects from around the world. In the salerooms is a treasure trove of items, and while some works may sell for prices that cause a media frenzy, many of the items offered at Christie's are affordable to even the novice collector. Insiders know that auctions are a great place to pick up exceptional pieces for sensible prices.

Teddy bears have been an exceptionally popular collecting subject over the last twenty years. Not only can they be wonderful historical objects, but everyone had a childhood teddy bear and so everyone can relate to them, with famous bears such as Aloysius, Pooh, Rupert and Paddington enhancing their appeal. Bears have now become serious (and sometimes expensive) collectables, and Christie's sells teddy bears in two auctions every year, sales that have become a highlight of many collectors' calendars.

The teddy bear has been hailed as the world's most popular toy and has been loved by children and adults alike for the past 100 years. *Christie's Century of Teddy Bears* traces the development of the bear from humble nursery companion to a valuable collector's item that dominates the soft-toy market and, since 1993, has commanded its own sales at Christie's auctioneers. This transformation is largely due to the growing number of adults who in recent decades have confessed to loving their old teddies and who have been prepared to pay increasingly large sums for vintage bears, particularly those made by Margarete Steiff GmbH, the company responsible for

below: *Steiff, James, 1999. Limited edition to mark the twenty-fifth anniversary of Christie's South Kensington.*

INTROD

creating the world's very first teddy bear in 1902. Today, some prices achieved by the rarest bears are beyond many collectors' pockets. Manufacturers have responded by producing limited edition replicas of sought-after lines exclusively for the collector's market, while those people who are only interested in original bears have targeted later models and toys produced by less popular manufacturers.

One unpleasant consequence of the now soaring popularity of the teddy bear is that in recent years forgeries have begun to appear on the market. Collectors are increasingly being put under pressure to part with large sums of money for bears that may not be what they seem. To avoid being deceived, it is always better to buy from a verified source – such as an auction house – and to be armed with as much knowledge of the subject as possible. To this end, *Christie's Century of Teddy Bears* charts the histories of the leading teddy bear manufacturers – such as Steiff, Ideal, Bing, Schuco, J.K. Farnell, Merrythought and Chad Valley – and the personalities that made these companies great, giving vital information on dates of

production and manufacturing methods that will help collectors to distinguish the genuine from the fake. Ultimately, however, people collect teddies because they are irresistibly drawn to them, and so this book tells the stories of individual bears who have touched the lives of their families and of all others to have come into contact with them.

Many soft-toy manufacturers have tried to come up with a toy to rival the popularity of the teddy bear, but all have failed. One explanation for the toy's phenomenal success is that it arrived at a time when there was a great need for a soft toy that appealed to both sexes, as dolls

UCTION

were seen as somewhat unsuitable for boys. Most teddy bears are themselves regarded as male, and in this book they have been referred to as 'he' apart from a few exceptions.

The bear's physical qualities must also have contributed to its success. Unlike most dolls of the period, which were fragile and vulnerable, the teddy could withstand rough-and-tumble treatment. Peter Bull, arctophile – derived from the Greek *arctos* (bear) and *philos* (love) – and author of *Bear with Me*, has offered his own explanation: 'A security blanket is far nearer to the bear in temperament, at least it affords comfort to a comparable degree. A doll seems to be (in my eyes) pretty vain and totally egotistic. The Teddy has physical qualities which make an immediate unselfish appeal. One knows instinctively that they are there to help and woe betide the person, of whatever age, suddenly deprived of their services.'

above: *Steiff, Teddy Baby, early 1930s. This cheerful bear was hugely popular during the 1930s.*

The same feelings were encapsulated by one of the leading British poets of the twentieth century, Sir John Betjeman, whose own teddy bear, Archibald Ormsby-Gore, he described as follows: 'Mr Archibald Ormsby-Gore has been with me as long as I can remember, he is about a foot high [approximately 30cm] when he is sitting down and is very patched. His eyes are wool, his ears and nose of some kind of cloth. Originally he was golden fur, but this only survives on his back and behind. He is very Protestant looking.' In 1960 Betjeman conveyed the importance of his teddy bear in his autobiographical poem *Summoned by Bells*:

Safe were those evenings of the pre-war world

When firelight shone on green linoleum;

I heard the church bells hollowing out the sky,

Deep beyond deep, like never-ending stars,

And turned to Archibald, my safe old bear,

Whose woollen eyes looked sad or glad at me,

Whose ample forehead I could wet with tears,

Whose half-moon ears received my confidence,

Who made me laugh, who never let me down,

I used to wait for hours to see him move,

Convinced that he could breathe. One dreadful day

They hid him from me as a punishment:

Sometimes the desolation of that loss

Comes back to me and I must go upstairs

To see him in the sawdust, so to speak,

Safe and returned to his idolater.

Since the first appearance of the teddy bear in 1902 children (and some adults) have realized that they are not just soft toys but companions that can share their triumphs and disasters, will comfort them in times of woe and join in adventures great and small. Some bears need more looking after than others: the fictional Aloysius in Evelyn Waugh's novel *Brideshead Revisited* caused his owner, Sebastian, constant headaches. On one occasion Sebastian wrote to his friend Charles: 'I've a good mind not to take Aloysius to Venice. I don't want him to meet a lot of horrid Italian bears and pick up bad habits.'

Edward Berkshire was much less of a handful than Aloysius, and yet he caused his original owner just as much heartache. In 1993 Christie's was asked by a charming eighty-year-old lady to find a

opposite: German, Edward, c.1914, pictured with his original owner. This photograph was used to date the bear.

new home for her glorious bear. She had no family of her own to pass Edward on to, and was concerned that one day he might be left alone. Edward's owner also parted with an enchanting photograph of herself, at one year old, with her bear, which was used to identify his country of origin – Germany – and year of birth – 1914.

In 1907, during the very early years of production of the teddy bear, Caroline Tickner, a Boston journalist with *New England Magazine*, encapsulated the appeal of the teddy bear when she wrote:

'The Teddy Bear has come to stay, so perfectly is his grizzled exterior adapted to fitting into the many chubby arms which extend to him. He is not only bear-like enough to lift him above juvenile criticism but he is possessed of those semi-human attributes which fit him eminently for youthful companionship. He is every inch a bear and yet he certainly embodies exactly the doll qualities which are demanded by the children of today. He is well-made and set up. His head really turns round and his legs are nicely adjustable. He has moreover that precious gift of true adaptability; he can be made to crawl, climb, stand or sit and in each pose he is not only delightfully himself but he also suggests to the imaginative owner whatever special being his fancy would have his teddy personify.'

To understand how such a paragon came about it is helpful to study the animal on which it was based, and its role in myth and folklore.

The bear family

The first teddy bears were based upon the grizzly bear. Since then, manufacturers have drawn on other kinds of bear for inspiration, particularly the American black bear, the polar bear and the panda.

The direct ancestors of the modern bear appeared on earth approximately two and a half million years ago. Members of this *Ursus* (bear) family later divided into three distinct evolutionary lines: two in Asia – the black and brown bears – and the third in Europe. The European bear, *Ursus spelaus* or the 'Cave Bear', became extinct thousands of years ago and its habitats were largely taken over by the brown bear. Today bears are found on four of the six continents (the exceptions being Antarctica and Australia), and can be divided into eight recognized groups.

The brown bear *(Ursus arctos)* is found throughout much of the northern hemisphere, including North America and Eurasia (particularly those countries that made up the former Soviet Union). The bears prefer to live in mountainous forested regions, large river valleys and open meadows. Their heavy shaggy coats vary in colour from black to cinnamon to golden, and the bears have a distinctive muscular hump on their shoulders. The grizzly is a large variety of brown bear found in North America. Its brown fur has cream or white tips that impart a grizzled appearance, hence the bear's name. Although the brown bear has been driven out of much of Europe, there are believed to be isolated populations still in Spain, France and Italy.

It is thought that polar bears *(Ursus maritimus)* are descended from brown bears, but they have adapted to survive in the extreme climate of the polar regions of the northern hemisphere, particularly Canada, the USA, Russia, Norway and Greenland. These excellent swimmers can be found on the oceanic ice floes of the northern shoreline, hunting for their favourite prey, the seal. Polar bears have thick white or yellowish fur, which acts as camouflage in their snowy environment and keeps out the cold both in water and on land. Beneath their fur their skin is black, a further heat-retaining attribute.

opposite: *Hans Long,* **Kragenbar,** *1930, oil on canvas, 100.2 x 68.5cm (39½ x 27in).*

The American black bear *(Ursus americanus)* is the most common bear in North America and is found from the northern tree limit of the Arctic down through most of Canada and the USA. It, too, likes forests with occasional open spaces. As its name suggests, this bear's fur is often black, although it can be various shades of brown. It can be distinguished from the brown bear by the absence of a hump on its shoulders.

The fourth group of ursine inhabitants of the Americas are spectacled bears *(Tremartos ornatus)*, so-called because their shaggy black coats are broken by distinctive white markings around the eyes, giving the bears the appearance of wearing glasses. There are thought to be less than 2,000 spectacled bears left in the world now that their preferred habitat, the cloud forests of South America, are quickly disappearing.

Deforestation policies across Asia are also devastating the bear populations of that continent. Asiatic black bears *(Ursus thibetanus)* live in the moist broad-leafed forests and brushland of central and east Asia, a habitat that is constantly being encroached upon by humans. This is one reason why the bears are now an endangered species. Another is that both their flesh and their bones are highly sought after by the Chinese for their supposed medicinal benefits. The bears have a very dense black coat, marked on the chest with a crescent- or moon-shaped patch of yellow or cream – hence their nickname, the Moon Bears of Tibet.

Sun bears *(Helarctos malayanus)* are the world's smallest bears. Deforestation in countries such as Burma,

Thailand, Laos, Kampuchea, Vietnam and Borneo has led to this bear, which is a good climber, coming close to extinction. They have short dense black fur with a yellowish U-shaped blaze on their chests.

In the late eighteenth century the pelt of a sloth bear *(Melursus ursinus)* was sent to Dr George Shaw at the British Museum, London, but he classified it wrongly as a sloth. When a live animal was sent to Britain in 1810 it was reclassified as a bear. Today there are between 7,000 and 10,000 sloth bears living in the tropical or subtropical regions of Sri Lanka, India, Bhutan, Nepal and Bangladesh, but their numbers are falling rapidly. Sloth bears are largely nocturnal animals with poor sight and hearing but an excellent sense of smell. They have undergone major evolutionary changes to the mouth and nose so that they are well adapted to suck out their favourite food – termites. Their long, shaggy, black coats are marked with a yellow or white 'V' on the chest.

Last, but by no means least, is the giant panda *(Ailuropoda melanoleuca)*, which until the late 1980s was classed with raccoons and lesser pandas but was then found through DNA testing to be closer to the bear family. These black and white bears with their distinctive eye patches exist at present only in cold damp coniferous forests in inland China, where they live almost exclusively off bamboo. Unfortunately

these forests are constantly being encroached upon by farmers and today there are only an estimated 700–1,000 giant pandas still wild in the world.

The koala *(Phascolarctos cinereus)* has been a popular model for teddy manufacturers, although this tree-dwelling Australian marsupial is actually not related to the bear family. Its teddy-like appearance nevertheless made it an obvious – and successful – choice for a soft toy.

Bears in myth and legend

For thousands of years bears have played an important part in the legends and folklore of countries around the world. The reasons why early humans were naturally fascinated by bears are complex, but are probably due in part to the fact that the animals were powerful adversaries that often walked upright (bears, like humans, have plantigrade feet, so that when they walk both heel and toes make contact with the ground). Some 75,000 years ago Neanderthal man elevated the now-extinct cave bear to a god, and ever since then bear cults have continued to exist alongside more orthodox religions. To this day the bear plays a significant role in the shamanistic rituals of the Lapps, the Inuit, North American Indians and the Ainu of Japan. Although some of these peoples still rely upon the bear for food, they respect the animals' power and skills and continue to honour its spirit once it is dead.

A she-bear was the symbol of Artemis, the goddess of the hunt in the Ancient Greek pantheon (known as Diana in Roman mythology). The link between animal and goddess was made explicit at Brauron in Attica, where young girls acted as bears in a festival dedicated to Artemis. The Roman poet Ovid told the story of Callisto, a nymph who served Artemis and who, like the goddess, had taken a vow of chastity. Callisto was seduced by Zeus, the father of the gods, who deceived her by taking the form of her mistress. The result of this union was a son, Arcas. Callisto was punished for her indiscretion by being turned into a she-bear either by Hera, the vindictive wife of Zeus, or by the unforgiving Artemis. She was later killed, possibly by her own son. Zeus then set Callisto into the heavens as the constellation of stars known today as the Great Bear. Arcas was turned into either the Little Bear or Arcturus, the brightest star in the northern hemisphere. The region of the bear stars, the Arctic, also takes its name from the Greek word for bear, *arktos*.

The bear also played a noteworthy part in the animal mythology of the Celtic world. The goddess Artio, whose name suggests she may have been related to Artemis, was represented by a she-bear. A bronze of the goddess holding fruit to feed a bear was found at Bern in Switzerland. (This city has strong links with the bear to this day: the animal is its mascot and bears have been kept in pits in Bern at the citizens' expense since 1480.) 'Art', meaning bear, is the root of early British names such as Artgenos, Arthgal and Arthur. The words '*matus*' (Gaulish) or '*math*' (Irish) likewise connote 'bear' and are discernible in the Gaelic name Mac Mathghamhna, meaning 'Son of a Bear'.

opposite: *Steiff, c.1920. A little white bear whose big brown eyes can easily fascinate.*

It is likely that the bear also loomed large in early Russian myths. It was certainly a popular figure in the folklore of that country by the twelfth century and was often used to symbolize the good qualities of the Russian common people. During the early eighteenth century, for example, the bear (often called Mishka) featured in many stories that illustrated the people's unease with the pro-European reforms of Peter the Great. It is possible that these warm feelings towards the animal were engendered by bearskin rugs, which gave welcome protection against Russia's freezing winters. Today bears continue to live in the vast forests that cover much of Russia and they remain a strong presence in the country's psyche. Indeed, Russia itself is often known as the Northern Bear.

One of the most famous medieval epics of Western Europe, *Reynard the Fox*, featured a bear amongst its cast of characters. Sir Bruin was one of the animals – along with Isegrim (a wolf) and Tybalt (a cat) – determined to bring Reynard to account for his many crimes. It is likely that the tale, set in a country ruled by King Nobel, a lion, was handed down verbally for centuries before being written down in the twelfth century. The earliest records of the story come from Alsace-Lorraine, and it is thought to have spread from there to Germany, France, the Low Countries and England. One of the most famous versions was produced in France between the mid-twelfth and the late thirteenth centuries. Some 500 years later the German poet Johann Wolfgang Goethe refashioned the epic.

One of the tales that features Sir Bruin tells how the bear tries to arrest Reynard and bring him before King Nobel for questioning. The fox tempts him to delay his mission, however, with the promise of a tree full of honey. Sir Bruin eagerly follows Reynard to a huge oak tree but is trapped inside and only narrowly escapes being killed by a mob of excited villagers. This episode, which shows the wily Reynard outwitting the greedy Sir Bruin, is a classic example from a tale that as a whole can be seen as a biting satire on the role of the church and nobility in medieval society.

Other tales to feature bears (or 'bruins' as they became known) had to wait until the nineteenth century before they were written down. The British poet and writer Robert Southey included a version of *The Three Bears* in a collection of essays and poetry published under the title *The Doctor* between 1834 and 1847. This popular children's story tells of how a girl called Goldilocks enters the bears' home while they are out and eats their porridge before falling asleep. The *Uncle Remus* fables, which were written down in the 1890s by the US author Joel Chandler Harris, have many similarities with the *Reynard the Fox* epic. Both describe how a smaller but more ingenious character triumphs; in the case of the *Uncle Remus* fables the hero, Bre'r Rabbit outwits a number of larger animals, including Bre'r Bear.

opposite: Steiff, Albert, c.1910. This Steiff centreseam bear is shown with his original owner in an image that sums up the bear's appeal.

The invention of childhood

Children, like all young creatures, are naturally playful, but the idea that children learn through play is a relatively modern one. Before the Reformation the Church looked upon children as potentially evil beings who could only be cleansed through baptism and confirmation, and this attitude pervaded society. Toys existed, but they were usually homemade dolls or games. Manufactured playthings tended to be aimed at adults rather than children and were generally entertaining novelties for the leisured classes. One of the first

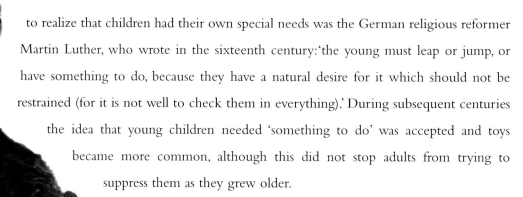

to realize that children had their own special needs was the German religious reformer Martin Luther, who wrote in the sixteenth century:'the young must leap or jump, or have something to do, because they have a natural desire for it which should not be restrained (for it is not well to check them in everything).' During subsequent centuries the idea that young children needed 'something to do' was accepted and toys became more common, although this did not stop adults from trying to suppress them as they grew older.

During the nineteenth century there was an increasing awareness of children's particular requirements, and this period saw a huge expansion in the production of toys, games and children's books. At the same time many countries introduced compulsory schooling for young children (in Britain the Education Act of 1880 required all children between the ages of five and ten to attend school), alongside laws to control and eventually eradicate child labour. Together these measures helped to ensure that by the start of the twentieth century many children had toys and the time to play with them.

The historical centre of toymaking

The religious Reformation of the sixteenth century not only encouraged a change of attitude towards children, but was also indirectly responsible for making Germany into the toy factory of the world. Woodcarving was a traditional occupation in the extensive forests of southern Germany, with most craftsmen producing religious works. After the Reformation the demand for such carvings (deemed idolatrous) declined and, over the next 200 years, was replaced by a market for wooden toys. The greatest concentration of toymakers was in five areas of southern Germany: Sonneberg,

Seiffen, Oberammergau, Berchtesgaden and the Groden Valley (now in Italy). At first carvers were based in their homes or in small community workshops, and sold their wooden toys to wholesalers who took them to markets in cities such as Nuremberg and Leipzig. Later, with the introduction of mass-production methods and the diversification into tinplate penny toys in the nineteenth century, factories were built closer to the markets. The toy centres developed specialisms: Nuremberg was renowned for its tin cars, boats and trains, while Sonneberg was known for its wooden toys and dolls.

Bear toys were produced throughout the nineteenth century, their appeal perhaps enhanced by the popularity of performing bears that could be seen in towns and cities across Europe and the USA during this period. These bears inspired the great French toy manufacturers, such as Roullet & Décamps and Gustave Vichy, to produce automata that could dance, beat a drum or growl, but such playthings were too expensive and fragile to be given to children. Much more suitable were the soft toys − including bears − that a German company founded by Margarete Steiff began to make towards the end of the century. It was these, the very first soft toys, that led to the birth of the teddy.

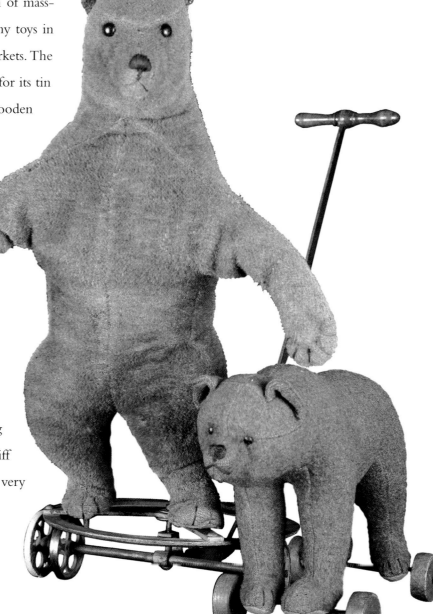

opposite: *This clockwork drummer bear was probably designed by Roullet & Décamps in around 1880.*
right: *Steiff bear on hind legs (1900) and pull-along bear.*

chapter 1

THE BIRTH OF THE BEAR

(1902–1904)

The story of how the teddy bear was born is a curious one, for the toy was invented in one continent but given its name in and adopted by another. In Germany Richard Steiff dedicated his early working years to making an irresistible plush bear, while in the USA the link was established between the toy and Theodore Roosevelt, a hunting-loving president, and the term 'teddy bear' was coined. And so the bear was safely delivered in late 1902 and his early popularity guaranteed. The story of the bear would be very different, however, were it not for the determination of a little girl born more than fifty years earlier. Apollonia Margarete Steiff, the aunt of Richard Steiff, was born on 24 July 1847. Her father, Friedrich, was a master builder in Giengen, a small town near Stuttgart. For the first eighteen months of her life Margarete was a healthy baby, but then she contracted polio. The virus, which attacks the brain and spinal cord, left her with a weakened right arm, a paralysed left foot and a partially paralysed right foot. These disabilities meant that she was to spend the rest of her life in a wheelchair.

Margarete's diary illustrates that, despite her difficulties, she was a happy and secure child who received enormous support from her devoted family. Every effort was made to find a cure for her, and for many years the Steiffs made endless trips to specialists and health spas. By 1857, however, when she was ten years old, Margarete had begun to accept her disability. Touching words in her diary read: 'It was a long time to spend searching for a cure. Finally I told myself that as God had obviously intended that I should not walk, I must accept His will.'

Perhaps as a distraction, she began to study the zither, and soon played the instrument well enough to give lessons. She was able to use the money to buy herself a sewing machine – probably the first one in Giengen, a town full of family-run dressmaking businesses – because she found sewing by hand difficult. Margarete became an expert seamstress and was soon receiving commissions throughout the neighbourhood. Having an income boosted her confidence enormously, and when a friend suggested that Margarete open her own dressmaking factory, she jumped at the chance: 'In 1877 I started … I opened my Felt Store.'

Her new business, the Felt Mail Order Co., was an immediate success, and soon she was able to employ a few people to help her produce felt petticoats and children's

below: *An early Steiff elephant pincushion, made by Margarete in around 1880 for her sister-in-law.*

clothes. As travel to European fashion shows and trade fairs was difficult for her, Margarete relied upon magazines to keep abreast of developments within the industry. One popular German magazine, *Modenwelt*, published do-it-yourself patterns that she often followed, including one of a small elephant she produced in felt as a pincushion for herself. Pleased with the result, she made others as gifts for her friends and family. Given that many people in Giengen were dressmakers, paying for such a knick-knack would have seemed absurd.

Until this time most toys for children had been manufactured out of hard materials, such as wood or tin. Dolls were popular, but their papier-mâché or porcelain heads and bodies stuffed with horsehair, were not comforting to cuddle. When they saw their mothers' felt elephant pincushions the children of Giengen claimed them for themselves, loving their size and tactile qualities. Margarete received an increasing number of requests for the elephants and eventually, on 29 December 1880, decided to start selling them. The first batch was snapped up, and soon soft toys, including dogs, camels, lions, monkeys and donkeys, formed the majority of her business. In 1886, for example, she sold 5,170 elephants.

In 1889 the company moved to larger premises in Muehlstrasse, and in 1892 produced its first catalogue, giving an overview of the entire range. In that year it also applied for a patent 'for the making of animals and other figures to serve as playthings'. The imitation that the patent was designed to avoid was something that would trouble the company a great deal in the future. The same year saw the launch of the first Steiff bear, which took the form of one of the many animals available in a skittles set. This little bear character proved to be extremely popular, and soon he featured in prime position as the kingpin of

above: *Apollonia Margarete Steiff, who spent most of her life in a wheelchair after contracting polio early in 1849.*

the skittles set. The Steiff bear had begun the journey that would see him perfected and established as the world's most popular soft toy. By 3 March 1893, when the Felt Toy Factory, Giengen, was entered in the trade register, the company had a turnover of 40,000 marks and employed four people full time, with a further ten homeworkers.

Margarete Steiff's brother Fritz played a vital role in the development of his sister's company, and all six of his sons – Richard, Franz, Paul, Otto, Hugo and Ernst – assisted greatly in building it into a flourishing concern. In 1897, just four years after it was registered, the company showed a turnover of 90,000 marks, and Margarete decided to have her own stand at the Leipzig Toy Fair. The person chosen as the family representative at the fair was her nephew Richard, Fritz's second son, who had just qualified from art school in Stuttgart and was to become, after his aunt, the second most influential figure in the history of the soft toy.

Richard Steiff's primary role in the company was to design and develop new toy lines. From the very beginning he seems to have been fascinated by the possibilities of a soft toy bear, and spent many hours trying to design one that would be attractive to children. To this end he made numerous sketches of bears in Stuttgart Zoo, circuses and animal shows. In fact his earliest models were

below: Steiff kingpin skittle in the shape of a bear, available on its own or as part of a set, c.1892.

rather too realistic, frightening rather than reassuring the young people for whom they were intended.

In the last years of the nineteenth century Richard Steiff designed a number of bears that, positioned on all fours and set on cast-iron wheels, were meant to be ridden or pulled. He also produced bears that stood upright on their hind legs. Although they were covered in mohair plush, these toys were not particularly huggable – some had internal metal frames, while others were so tightly stuffed with woodwool that they felt solid. Then, in 1902, he devised a series of string-jointed movable animals, including a bear – the first such toy in the world. The first bear prototypes met with a cool response from Margarete, who thought that their brown plush coats, woven from mohair to resemble real fur, were too expensive. Richard persevered, however, determined to develop a sample that would convince his aunt.

Although there are no known surviving examples of Steiff's first commercial bear-doll, production details and catalogue images in the Steiff archive reveal some valuable information about how he looked, as does his name. Following the system used to name subsequent bears, this Bär 55 PB would have been 55cm (22in) tall when seated, hence the number in his title. The letters that follow signify he was made of *Plusch* (plush) and was *Beweglich* (movable). He had a long pointed muzzle, a hump at the top of his back, a short plump torso, large feet and long

opposite: *The house in Giengen where Margarete Steiff spent her childhood.*

right: *Margarete Steiff's nephews (from the top): Ernst, Otto, Hugo, Franz, Richard and Paul. All six worked for the family business at some point.*

So Bär 55 PB, the very first jointed bear, created in 1902, made his public debut at the Leipzig Toy Fair in March 1903. Here, too, he received a cool reception – indeed, he was referred to as a 'stuffed misfit'. Yet at the end of the fair, when the Steiff brothers had already started nailing down the sample boxes, Hermann Berg, chief buyer for the toy department of New York wholesaler George Borgfeldt & Co., appeared. He had been searching the fair in vain for new ideas, and when his eyes fell upon the toy bears he immediately saw their potential and ordered 3,000 of them.

Paul Steiff, another nephew, was in New York in 1903 monitoring exactly which Steiff samples had arrived from Giengen. He kept a diary from which we learn that sales staff were showing samples of Bär 55 PB to retail stores in New York soon after the Leipzig Toy Fair. Curiously, no record exists of Berg's 3,000 Bär 55 PBs, including Richard Steiff's prototype, after they were shipped from Germany. None has so far come to light, which may be due to the frailty of the string-jointing, but collectors live in hope that one day a Bär 55 PB will be unearthed.

Bär 55 PB had been born, but he had yet to be given the name by which he is known around the world today. German by birth, he was at first referred to as Petsy (after *Meister Petz*, an old-fashioned term for bruin). To become a household name he would need the services of the 26th president of the USA: Theodore Roosevelt (1858–1919), known as Teddy to his friends, was born in New York, of Dutch and Scottish descent. He, like Margarete Steiff, was ill as a child – he suffered from asthma. As a young man he was a fitness fanatic, and as part of the macho image he cultivated he became a dedicated big-game hunter. After studying at Harvard he spent two years on a cattle ranch in Dakota before becoming leader of the New York

curved arms that extended beyond his legs when he was seated (early Steiff bears were made so that they could stand on all fours). A flexible jointing system enabled his head and limbs to be moved. His nose was of sealing wax and had finely carved nostrils, and his eyes were black boot buttons made out of moulded woodpulp. These were attached to either footwear or bears by metal hooks, which were pushed into the flat button backs before they dried.

legislature (1884) and later president of the New York Police Board (1895–7). Influential in Republican circles, he was assistant secretary to the US Navy when in 1898 he raised and commanded 'Roosevelt's Rough Riders' in the Spanish American War in Cuba, returning to become governor of New York State (1898–1900). Appointed vice-president of the USA in 1901, he became president later that year when William McKinley was shot dead by the anarchist Leon F. Czolgosz in Buffalo, New York.

Roosevelt's passion for hunting was well known – by the time he became president he had written several books on the subject – so when, in November 1902, he was in the American South to arbitrate in a border dispute between the states of Louisiana and Mississippi, it was natural for him to take time off to go bear hunting on the Mississippi Delta. After four days of hunting Roosevelt had still made no kill and on the afternoon of 14 November 1902, his embarrassed hosts searched the woods for a bear for the president to shoot, and eventually flushed out and tethered an elderly bear. Roosevelt was contemptuous; he refused to shoot such a pitiful sitting target. His humanity, though, did not extend to saving the bear's life – it was dispatched by a hunter's knife.

The press was in attendance and the incident was reported. Clifford K. Berryman, as cartoonist for the *Washington Post*, went one step beyond straight reportage, explicitly linking the episode to the purpose behind the president's visit. He drew a cartoon captioned 'Drawing the Line in Mississippi', depicting Roosevelt, hand raised, refusing to shoot at close range a small, tethered and terrified bear. When the cartoon was published in the *Washington Post* two days later it attracted widespread attention in Washington and New York. It seems that the term 'teddy bear' was already in existence by the end of

above: *Richard Steiff's sketchbook showing his life-drawings of bears.*

right: *Theodore Roosevelt, pictured on Christmas Day 1916.*

the same month: Berryman himself drew a pen portrait of Theodore Roosevelt and a small bear, next to which he wrote the words 'Teddy Bear Nov. 1902'. This makes it very likely that it was the cartoonist himself who coined the term. Berryman drew other versions of the original and used the bear as a motif in several later political cartoons in which he charted the remainder of Roosevelt's presidency.

opposite: *Clifford K. Berryman, 'Drawing the Line in Mississippi', 1902,* **Washington Post.**

It is not known, however, who first applied the name to the soft toy, although there are those who claim to have done so, which brings us to the final figures in the early history of the teddy bear: Morris Michtom, a Russian émigré, and his wife, Rose. This couple, who ran a stationery and novelty store on Thompson Avenue in Brooklyn, New York, saw the cartoon and, so the story goes, decided to harness the publicity it caused by making a stuffed toy bear and placing him in their window beside a card that read 'Teddy's Bear'. He sold almost immediately, as did the others Rose made to replace him.

Unlike Steiff's 55 PB, which was the culmination of years of research and development by the world's leading soft-toy manufacturer, the Michtoms' first bear seems to have been the result of a flash of inspiration. As such, it is extremely unlikely that he would have looked like his German counterpart (the original Michtom bear, too, has been lost). This bear has often been described as having been similar to a rag doll in design, and certainly it is highly improbable that the Michtoms would have chosen independently the same materials, design of bear and jointing system as Richard Steiff.

No evidence exists to confirm whether or not it was indeed Michtom who first described the toy as Teddy's Bear. Nevertheless, whatever the folklore surrounding this part of the story, there is no doubt that the demand for Teddy's Bears soon became too great for the Michtoms to handle on their own. Butler Brothers, a Brooklyn-based wholesaler with interests in plush-producing mills, proceeded to buy up the entire bear stock from the Michtom's shop. This collaboration resulted in the foundation of the Ideal Novelty and Toy Co. – the first US teddy-bear manufacturer.

Such was the impact of Berryman's Roosevelt cartoons that the number of teddy bears bought in the USA increased steadily. But few could have predicted the craze that would soon ignite the country and spread to the rest of the world, stretching the production capabilities of toy manufacturers to their limits.

DRAWING THE LINE IN MISSISSIPPI

chapter 2

THE BEAR GROWS UP

(1905–1919)

President Roosevelt was quick to recognize the appeal of the teddy bear and was to use him as his mascot for the rest of his political life. Indeed, during the 1904 presidential election campaign bears produced by the recently formed Ideal Novelty and Toy Co. were handed out to potential voters. The bears were only 15cm (6in) tall and had large round staring eyes, known as googly or Goo-Goo eyes. This style of eye was popular on dolls of the day, and probably derived from cartoons. A wealth of other memorabilia – both official and unofficial – featuring the president and his furry companion followed, including badges, lapel pins, and china and moulded glass plates. Roosevelt's second term in office (1905–09) saw a phenomenal demand for teddy bears in the USA, although this was

below: Bears were a common motif during the teddy craze, decorating items ranging from tea sets to jewellery boxes.

probably an indication of the public's satisfaction with the toy rather than with the president. Manufacturers sprang up in response, producing not only the bears themselves but also teddy-related games, cards, sweets, money banks and items of clothing – the list was endless. Interestingly, when supporters of Roosevelt's successor, William Taft, tried to replicate the phenomenon during the 1909 presidential election, they failed. The teddy bear had captured the public's heart and was not to be ousted by an upstart marsupial called Billy Possum.

It was not long before bears started to feature in books and comicstrips. Among the earliest were the human-sized and impeccably dressed Teddy-B and Teddy-G. This pair, known as the Roosevelt Bears, were the inspiration of teacher and journalist Seymour Eaton. Their exciting adventures, which were told in pictures

and verse, started appearing in US newspapers in 1905, and were swiftly followed by four hugely successful books. The stories prompted numerous spin-offs, including the production in Germany and the USA of dressed teddy bears.

In 1906 the toy became independent of the president when the term 'teddy bear', rather than Teddy's bear, first appeared in the US toy trade journal *Playthings*. It was in that same year that the teddy-bear craze really took a grip on the USA. Hundreds of songs were composed about the little bears, including, in 1907, John W. Bratton's 'The Teddy Bears' Picnic' (the lyrics to which were not added, however, until 1930), and reports came from all over the country of shops failing to keep up with the enormous demand for the cuddly toys.

Perfectly placed to meet this demand was the Ideal Novelty and Toy Co. By 1907 the company required larger premises and relocated, still within Brooklyn, to 311–17 Christopher Avenue. Soon afterwards it advertised in *Playthings* magazine describing itself as 'the largest bear manufacturers in the country'. Under the headline 'Why send to Europe for your Jointed Animals when you can buy them right here at half the price?', it claimed to produce 'an exact reproduction of the foreign model'. Such an open admission of its debt to Steiff would not be repeated once the German company began protecting its designs in the courts.

The first Ideal teddy bears, although of high quality, were not labelled, making them difficult to identify today. Fortunately the bears were illustrated in contemporary *Playthings* catalogues, so their appearance is known. Further details on their design and manufacture have been gleaned through study of an early bear presented to the Smithsonian Institute in Washington DC. Typically the bears had broad foreheads, large ears set wide apart and wedge-shaped muzzles, giving the head a triangular appearance. Their noses were sometimes made from broadcloth – a fine closely woven fabric – but were more usually stitched. The coat was normally of short golden mohair plush and the stuffing was woodwool (long

above: *Ceramic milk pitcher by Buffalo Pottery decorated with scenes from the Roosevelt Bears books.*

right: *Ideal Novelty and Toy Co., c.1910. Although unlabelled, this bear's triangular shaped head and slightly pointed paw pads are typical of Ideal.*

shavings of a softwood such as birch). Like the first Steiff bears, early Ideal teddies tended to have plump bodies with a realistic hump at the top of the back and long, curved arms. Unique to the US company, however, were the bear's oval pointed footpads. Most of the bears had black boot-button eyes, although the company was experimenting with glass eyes, possibly under the guidance of Abraham Katz, a friend of the Michtoms who joined the company as co-chairman in 1912 and greatly influenced production and design matters.

To fulfil an increase in demand for teddy bears, companies sprang up throughout the country. A second firm from this period to produce bears that have withstood the test of time was the Bruin Manufacturing Co. While an accurate date for the company's founding has yet to be established, its teddies appeared in *Playthings* as early as 1907. BMC was based at 497 Broome Street, New York City. The faces of its high-quality bears had a similar shape to those produced by Ideal – with wide foreheads and pointed muzzles – but the ears of BMC bears, though wide set, tended to be small, and their golden mohair plush coats were often longer than those of their Ideal competitors. More importantly, when it comes to identification, the Bruin Manufacturing Co. securely labelled each of its bears with a blue and red woven label with the letters 'B.M.C.' embroidered in gold thread. The company ceased business in 1908; because it produced teddies for such a short period of time, its bears are highly sought after in today's market.

Many of the manufacturers that emerged during these first years were short-lived. Some failed because competition became too fierce; others may have had difficulty sourcing materials. Like BMC, the Aetna Toy Animal Co.

(formerly known as Keystone Bears) produced high-quality teddy bears using the very best materials available, for a similarly short period of time. Little is known about the company, which advertised in *Playthings* for only two years, from 1906 to 1908. Its traditional mohair plush teddy bears had triangular faces with large flat ears and glass or boot-button eyes. The name Aetna within an oval outline was stamped in blue on the bears' feet. Aetna is also known to have made a two-tone bear wearing a wide collar and a pointed cap.

left: *Bruin Manufacturing Co., 1907–8. Bears produced by this short-lived company were all marked with embroidered labels.*

Another short-lived manufacturer producing in the early 1900s was Hecla. All makers during this period owed a debt to Steiff, which was leading the field in both Europe and the USA with its innovative designs, but Hecla's teddy bears displayed a remarkable resemblance to those of the German company. The bears were made with imported German mohair and were often assembled by experienced German toymakers, but somehow they lacked the Steiff magic. The public was not convinced and production was abandoned after only a few years.

Columbia Teddy Bear Manufacturers, a company founded before 1910, used the name of explorer Christopher Columbus to emphasize its Americanness,

*below: The rivalry between American and German manufacturers is revealed in this advertisement from **Playthings**.*

perhaps in an attempt to woo customers away from 'the foreign model'. As with so many firms dating from this period, information about its design and production methods is scarce. It is known that it was based at 145–9 Center Street, New York City, and that it used imported material including mohair (mainly from Germany) to make its bears. Perhaps the only bear that can be confidently attributed to Columbia is its Laughing Roosevelt Bear, which was advertised in a 1907 edition of *Playthings*. When the stomach of this novel toy was squeezed, the bear's mouth opened to reveal two white glass fangs set into the front of the lower jaw. On release the bear's mouth closed, and the teeth were concealed within holes in the wooden upper jaw. Although he was supposed to be laughing, the bear had a rather fierce expression, which was hardly ideal in a soft toy. The fangs, too, were potentially dangerous and would surely have caused parents some concern. For whatever reason, few of the bears have survived and today they are highly sought after by collectors.

Also based in New York City – at Broadway, Department 1 – was the Strauss Manufacturing Co. Inc. This firm's core business was the production of games and novelty toys – indeed, it advertised itself as the 'Toy King of New York'. Tempted by the bear mania that was spreading throughout the USA in the early 1900s, it introduced teddies to its range, applying its experience in the novelty toy market to the making of its bears. Among the models that resulted from this fusion was the most unusual Self-Whistling Bear (1907), whose mechanism was activated by tipping the bear upside down. Musical bears also joined the range, with ingenious movements built in their backs and operated by fixed porcelain handles.

The Strauss teddy bears were notably similar to those produced by Steiff at the time, but with one significant difference: Strauss bears often had red embroidered noses, mouths and claws. Although the bears were of good quality, ultimately Strauss proved to be yet another short-lived US company hoping to cash in on the toy's popularity. Today, because of the age of the bears and the brevity of the company's existence, Strauss teddies are extremely rare.

The Fast Black Skirt Co. of 109 East 124th Street, New York City, was also known for its novelty bears. Perhaps its most famous product was the Electric Bright Eye Teddy Bear, whose mechanism was explained in *Playthings*: 'Shake the right paw and the eyes light up with electricity in either red or white.' The bear was available in various sizes from 38cm to 91cm (15in to 3ft), depending on whether buyers wanted to display their new friend in their parlour or their automobile. Such considerations suggest that Electric Bright Eye was being marketed at adults rather than children. It is certainly true that at the height of the teddy-bear craze the toy was being depicted on many items for grown-ups, including chinaware and silverware, biscuit and sweet tins, stationery and paperweights – in fact anything that could be decorated was decorated with bears.

As well as the 'top-drawer' US manufacturers that tried to emulate the quality standards set by Steiff, there were numerous smaller firms, whose names are now unknown, mass-producing cheap and cheerful bears. These toys are today referred to as stick bears because of their thin bodies and crudely jointed rigid limbs. Produced in very large numbers they appear frequently in salerooms today, but their cheapness when first available is reflected in the small sums paid for them today.

left: *The American Made Stuffed Toy Co., c.1917. When turned on, the eyes of this battery-powered bear lit up.*

right: *American stick bear, 1910s. The maker of this patriotic red, white and blue teddy is unknown.*

below: *Columbia Teddy Bear Manufacturers, Laughing Roosevelt Bear, c.1907, seen with its mouth open.*

B. M. C.
(Trade-Mark)

The B. M. C. Zoo

Offers the Most Perfect Menagerie of Stuffed Animals ever shown in Toyland

A full line of Bears, Rabbits, Cats, Dachsunds, Elephants, etc. Best plush--superb workmanship and finish. **With Imported Voices**

Our Bears Excel the Imported

We have in preparation a line of Bear Outfits and Accessories that will create a sensation

A Group of
B. M. C. Playmates

BRUIN MFG. CO.,
497 Broome Street,
Phone 6902 Spring, New York City

Selling Agents:
The Strobel & Wilken Co.,
591 Broadway, N. Y.

left: *This advert for BMC from 1907 reveals that the company were working on a line of dressed bears.*

STEIFF'S BÄRENJAHRE AND BEYOND

The main market for teddy bears may have been the USA, but it was Richard Steiff in Germany who perfected the design of the bear and whose work was imitated by other manufacturers around the world. On 13 July 1903 the Felt Toy Factory registered the pattern for Bär 55 PB, the first jointed bear, at the court in Heidenbeim, but this did not mean that Richard stopped trying to perfect the design. On the contrary, he reassessed all elements of the bear – size, shape, joints and mohair – and on 5 March 1904 an improved thread-jointed model was registered as Bär 35 PB. Margarete Steiff was still worried that the bear might fail, but her fears proved groundless. Order books soon filled and by the end of 1904 Steiff had sold 12,000 bears. That year Paul and Richard Steiff were invited to decorate the entrance to the Toy Hall at the St Louis World Expo in the USA. Both the resultant display and the company itself were a huge success at the fair: Margarete and Richard were awarded gold medals for their industry, and thereafter decorative tableaux were lent to large department stores around the world for advertising purposes.

It was at this stage, when the scale of the bear's success was beginning to be imagined, that Steiff had the foresight to design and apply a trademark to its products. It began by attaching cardboard labels to its bears, but these proved too fragile to withstand the rough treatment meted out by some of its young customers. Then Franz Steiff came up

left: *Steiff, Bär 28 PB, c.1904. Although this rod-jointed bear has obviously been well loved, his original sealing wax nose remains intact.*

with the brilliantly simple idea of attaching a small nickel-plated button to the left ear of every bear produced. The first buttons, introduced on 1 November 1904, were embossed with an elephant with an S-shaped trunk, and the trademark Button-In-Ear was registered on 20 December 1904. There followed a short period when blank buttons were used, before those embossed 'STEIFF' were introduced on 13 May 1905. The Steiff Button-In-Ear was a genuine mark of quality, and as such, like the bears it decorated, it was soon being imitated by European and US manufacturers, provoking a series of costly and time-consuming legal battles.

Steiff continued to manufacture Bär 55 PB until 1 February 1904. His replacement, brought in towards the end of 1904, was the rod-jointed Bär 28 PB, which could be moved by means of a system of metal rods that ran through his body. Bär 28 PB had a horizontal seam across the top of his head, small round ears, a long shaved muzzle ending in a nose made from sealing wax (complete with finely carved nostrils) and large narrow feet.

Bär 28 PB was well received, but Richard Steiff was still not satisfied with the bear's appearance – and neither was his aunt. He continued to improve on the design until, in early 1905, he was able to present Margarete with Bär 35 PAB (the A referring to Angeschiebt or disc-jointed). She was enchanted and called the new model Bärle (an affectionate German term used to denote something or someone dear).

Bärle was everything Richard had dreamed of and Margarete had desired. He was available in white, light brown or dark brown plush, was soft filled with excelsior (a US tradename for wood-wool) and kapok, and jointed with card discs. This method of jointing, in which the slippery surfaces of two circles of card held by a cotter pin

allow smooth rotation in one plane, is still used today. In 1905, customers could choose from seven sizes, and this was increased to fourteen in 1910. With his small round ears, black boot-button eyes (black glass button eyes were introduced in around 1908 on special orders only), shaved muzzle and stitched nose, plump body and large feet, he had the kind of appeal that few children – or adults – could resist. Some of the bears came with squeeze boxes or squeakers inside that were made from coiled spring sandwiched between two round pieces of card or wood held together by a strip of oilcloth. When the bear was squeezed in the correct place the spring was compressed, forcing air through a reed to produce a grunt.

below: Richard Steiff, pictured holding the grey mohair prototype for Bärle that he designed in 1905.

above: *The first Steiff Button-in-Ear, an elephant with an 'S'-shaped trunk, was used from 1904 to 1905.*

left: *Steiff, c.1906. This early light brown Bärle has black boot-button eyes.*

The perfected 1905 bear was an instant success – in the year following his release some 400,000 teddies were sold. Demand was so great that Steiff was forced to take extra measures to avoid any wastage of mohair plush. Six whole heads were cut from each length of material, with a seventh head cut in two halves. This meant that every seventh bear had a seam running down the centre of his face. Today the centre-seam teddy is particularly prized by collectors for its added rarity.

A new business structure was needed to run the rapidly expanding firm, so on 30 May 1906 the Felt Toy Factory was reregistered as a private limited company, Margarete Steiff GmbH, with four of Margarete's nephews – Richard, Paul, Otto and Hugo – as managing directors. In 1907 some 975,000 bears were made, a number that has yet to be bettered – indeed, the years 1903 to 1908 are known as the *Bärenjahre*, or Bear Years, at Steiff. Work had begun on a new factory in Giengen in 1902, but now it was further extended to accommodate the 400 employees.

From early on Steiff had been particularly good at developing foreign markets. During his year in New York (1902–3) Paul Steiff had run a showroom promoting the company's products, but it was his brother Otto (joining the company in 1900) who had responsibility for distribution and advertising. Under Otto's guidance a network of warehouses around the world was established to service the company's mail-order business. He also spent time abroad, encouraging Steiff's burgeoning overseas staff – by 1907 there were 1,800 people working for the company worldwide – and nurturing the markets in England, France and particularly the USA, from where most of the orders were coming. Later he oversaw the opening of branches in New York and Paris.

It was during these boom years, when competition was fierce, that Steiff produced some of its most memorable teddy bears. In 1907 it had introduced a hotwater-bottle teddy bear, possibly inspired by a particularly harsh winter the previous year. The 25cm (10in) bear had an opening in his mohair plush body into which could be inserted a firmly sealed tin of boiling water, and was padded so as not to scald his owner. What better for a small child to snuggle up to on a cold night? Nowadays such novelty hotwater bottles can be found in pharmacies every winter, but it would seem that Steiff's bear was ahead of its time – only

above: *Steiff, Will, c.1906. Like Teddy Girl, Will is a superb example of an early cinnamon Steiff.*

above: *The innovative glass and steel buildings of Steiff's factory in Giengen in 1908, the year they were completed.*

sound produced. When the bear was tilted a weighted bellows was compressed, forcing air through a reed and emitting a growl.

Another innovative design was the Snap-a-Part – a bear that could be pulled to pieces but then easily reassembled (something that any parent of a destructive toddler will instantly recognize as a winner). As with every new design, Steiff sent the Snap-a-Part to the patent office. But as Carl Pfenning had already invented the snap-fastener in 1895 – for gentlemen's trousers rather than toys – the patent request was rejected. The wonderful Roly-Poly Bear accompanied the Snap-a-Part range. With his spherical body that wobbled from side to side when touched, he, too, offered durability and endless fun to young children.

During this enthusiastic time of continuous new releases, bright colours were introduced, bringing a new dimension to the Steiff range. Today these captivating bears are prized pieces in any collection, but initially they were received with limited interest and even less admiration. Perhaps most children wanted ordinary teddy bears and shied away from the exotic looking.

This attitude is well illustrated by the story of Elliot, believed to be the only blue mohair 1908 Steiff ever made. When Steiff introduced its brightly coloured bears in 1908 it offered them as samples to its long-standing accounts. The buyer for Harrods department store in London at the time was the only person to be offered a blue bear. He took one look at Elliot and rejected him out of hand, considering that blue was not an appropriate colour for a bear and therefore he would not sell. A contemporary blank order form shows that no orders were made, so Elliot was a genuine one-off, a sample for a line that was never commercially manufactured.

ninety examples were manufactured between 1907 and 1914 before the model was withdrawn. Consequently these bears are highly sought after by collectors around the world, and if they come complete with hotwater bottle they can fetch impressive figures at auction.

By 1908 Steiff had accepted the US name for its toys, and all Bärles from then onwards were catalogued as teddy bears. That same year the company introduced Maulkorb Bär, literally Muzzled Bear, which wore a leather harness similar to those used to restrain dancing bears in Europe and the USA during the nineteenth century. This bear had an internal voicebox known as a growler because of the

One of the most famous coloured Bärles was Alfonzo. a red 33cm (13in) bear given to Princess Xenia of Russia by her father, Grand Duke George Mikhailovich, in 1908. The princess named the bear Alfonzo, and her nanny, Miss Ball (known fondly by the family as 'Nanabell'), made him a cotton Cossack tunic and trousers. Their early life together was spent in Horax House, a palace close to her cousin the Tsar's villa in the Crimea.

Soon they became inseparable, so when the ten-year-old princess went to London in July 1914, to spend her summer holidays at Buckingham Palace, she naturally took Alfonzo with her. The outbreak of World War I in August 1914 prevented their return to Russia, so they became guests of Queen Alexandra at Marlborough House. When revolution broke out at home it became obvious that their stay was to be a lengthy one, so they moved to their own London house in Chester Square.

Princess Xenia must have been desolate when she heard the news that Tsar Nicholas II had been forced to abdicate on 17 March 1917, and even more so when he was shot with his entire family at Yekaterinburg by the Red Guards in July 1918. Her father, who had remained in Russia, survived the initial slaughter but was assassinated in St Petersburg in 1919. Alfonzo was the only memento of her father that the princess had taken from Russia, and this terrible event made the bear even more important to her.

In 1921 Princess Xenia married William Leeds, an American whose father was known as the 'Tin Croesus'

left: *Steiff, Hotwater-bottle Teddy, c.1907. The canister was filled with hot water and put inside the bear, which was then laced up.*

the bear grows up

right: *Steiff, a Roly-Poly Bear dating from around 1909, held by a cinnamon bear from the same period.*

left: *Steiff, Alfonzo, c.1908. Princess Xenia's red mohair companion, wearing the Cossack tunic made for him by the princess's nanny, Miss Bell.*

below: *Steiff, Elliot, c.1908. The only known blue mohair Steiff of the period, Elliot was rejected by the buyer for Harrod's department store in London.*

thanks to the fortune he had made from mining that metal. They moved to New York and, naturally, Alfonzo went too. When the princess died in 1965 Alfonzo was inherited by her daughter, Nancy, who kept him with her until his sale at Christie's in 1989.

Teddy bears clothed in splendid outfits fared better than their colourful cousins when they were introduced – possibly the success of Seymour Eaton's Roosevelt Bears

fuelled a demand for dressed bears. They were used extensively in advertising campaigns, and the complexity of their wardrobes – complemented by the quality of the clothing, which was equal to that of the bears themselves – proved remarkably popular with the public.

On 9 May 1909 production was halted – a rare occurrence – and flags in Giengen were flown at halfmast, when the company's founder, Margarete Steiff, died aged sixty-one. Her enormous contribution to the industry meant that toy manufacturers around the world mourned her passing. But it was in her home town that her death was felt most keenly. Her friends, family and employees had all benefited from her many acts of kindness, as well as her visionary business sense. Delivering the funeral address three days later the pastor described how she provided many employees with bread and work, 'and the hours were not too long or the work too hard', as well as giving comfort and aid to the weak, crippled, poor and needy.

Margarete had trained her nephews well, however, and they ensured that the company remained at the forefront of the industry, its name synonymous with quality. The novelty designs continued with a range of irresistible mechanical bears, developed by Hugo Steiff, who had studied engineering at Mannheim. Probably the most famous of the range was the Purzel Bär (Somersaulting Bear), which was introduced in 1909. This teddy had a clockwork motor that was wound up by twisting the bear's arm. Once released the bear would tumble forwards across the ground.

left: *Margarete Steiff (1847–1909) is pictured with a 'perfected' white teddy bear in this painting by Otto Neubrand.*

During this period the Steiffs were involved in making a German film featuring their toys. 'Steiff toys star in movie!' one newspaper article reported. The creative artist involved in the film's production was a bright young Prussian called Albert Schlopsnies. Richard Steiff admired the work Schlopsnies did on the film and felt he could bring fresh ideas to the company, so in 1910 he invited him to join it. Schlopsnies wished to remain self-employed but agreed to become an artistic advisor. The other members of the management were horrified by Richard's inviting an outsider into their highly successful family firm, but he managed to convince them that their toys would benefit from Schlopsnies's creative input.

Richard's gamble paid off. In 1910 the toy industry was once again captivated when Steiff launched Schlopsnies's Marionette Series, including the Pantom Bär. This thrilling puppet, whose name derives from the word pantomime, was operated by strings attached to his limbs. The bear also had a pull-cord voicebox, which was particularly effective if the puppeteer was out of sight.

One of Schlopsnies's main responsibilities was to produce moving tableaux for department-store windows and toy fairs around the world, which he did so imaginatively that he made the name of Steiff more famous than ever. During the autumn of 1910 the Wertheim department store in Berlin's Potsdamer Platz was the setting for his model of the Circus Sarrasani. With its clowns, acrobats and performing animals it delighted the city and began a tradition of showpieces that endures today. It may also have provided the inspiration for his Circus Series, released in the mid-1930s.

On a more sombre note, when one of the worst seafaring tragedies of the century occurred in 1912 Steiff paid its respects by honouring the dead with a special edition of bears. On 14 April 1912 the passenger liner *Titanic* was speeding towards New York on her maiden transatlantic voyage when, at 11.40pm, she struck an iceberg off the Grand Banks of Newfoundland, Canada. Water poured through a 90m (300ft) gash below the waterline, and in less than three hours the liner had sunk. White Star Line,

above: *Steiff, Purzel Bär (Somersaulting Bear), c.1909. A much imitated clockwork toy.*

London within weeks of the disaster. Clearly touching a chord, they sold out quickly.

Five years previously Steiff had produced a sample black bear that had met with a very cool reception. Perhaps buyers thought that, with their black boot-button eyes glinting on orange felt, the teddies were too ferocious-looking to appeal to children. Or maybe their rich black mohair coats were considered too funereal. For whatever reason, the bears were not commercially produced in 1907, although a prototype from that year remains in the archives. After the initial production of *Titanic* bears, a further 161 black bears were made between 1917 and 1919, making the total number produced 655. Today they are some of the most sought-after bears in the world.

Steiff continually drew on events and myths from around the world for inspiration. In 1913 it produced Dolly Bär in time for the US presidential election, incorporating the red, white and blue of the Stars and Stripes banner in the design. That same year saw the introduction of the Record Series, including Record Teddy, a 25cm (10in) bear seated on a metal chassis above four wooden wheels. When the light brown plush teddy was pulled forwards his arms and head would move as if he was rowing, and he would emit a growl. Other wheeled novelty toys offered by Steiff during this period included traditional-looking bears on all fours with pull-along cords. These ranged in height from 17cm to 60cm (7in to 2ft); the smaller ones could be taken for walks on their leads, while the larger versions provided delightful transport for small children.

Such innovation, however, was of necessity suspended in 1914: with the outbreak of World War I the bottom fell out of the toy market. Germany's borders were closed,

which owned the ship, had considered the *Titanic* unsinkable and so had not provided enough liferafts. The death toll was horrendous: 1,513 people died, mainly men who had allowed women and children to go first, and those travelling lower class, who were hampered in their attempts to reach the liferafts.

above: *Steiff, Dolly Bär known as Gilbert, 1913. This teddy was made for a US presidential election.*

When news of the catastrophe reached England the whole country was plunged into mourning. Steiff responded by producing 494 black bears, which were displayed in shop windows throughout

left: *Pantom Bear and Pantom Artilleryman from Steiff's Marionette Series of 1910 are seen here being manipulated by their creator, Albert Schlopsnies.*

A TEUTONIC TALENT FOR TEDDIES

In spite of the reverses caused by World War I, during the early twentieth century Germany remained the toymaking capital of the world, so it was not long before others tried to replicate Steiff's success. This was a hugely creative period in the teddy bear's history, with hundreds of manufacturers, both new and old, producing bears of all shapes and sizes. Each exciting new product launched on the market was quickly taken up and imitated or improved by others in the industry. Workers would move from one company to another, taking with them their skills, ideas and designs, and sometimes even the products themselves.

Steiff's principal competitor in Europe during the early years of teddy-bear manufacture was Gebrüder Bing. Founded in Nuremberg in southern Germany in 1863 by brothers Ignaz and Adolphe Bing, the company began as a wholesaler of kitchenware and tinware. In 1881 the brothers turned to toymaking, and had soon set up the Bing Brothers' Nuremberg Toy Factory in Karolinestrasse. There they produced all manner of tinplate and enamelled toys, including trains, boats and automobiles, many of which were mechanized. Bing produced for the top end of the market and sold its wares in showrooms throughout Europe. In 1895 they changed the company name to Nuremberg Metal and Enamelware Works, and that same year Adolphe, after thirty-two years in partnership, left the company. By the early 1900s Bing was one of the largest toy manufacturers in the world, and indeed its catalogue for 1906 describes an impressive firm of around 3,000 employees and showrooms in Hamburg, Berlin, London, Paris, Milan and Amsterdam.

which meant that exports to countries such as the USA, France and Britain became impossible. Imports of raw materials, including spun mohair from the north of England, were also cut off, but the shortage was not really felt until 1917. Richard, Paul and Hugo Steiff were called up for military service, while their factory was required to produce essential war supplies. Some toys were also made, including soldier dolls in German, Belgian, Austrian, Turkish, Italian and Russian uniforms, but there is no record of dressed teddy bears.

above: *Steiff, Record Teddy, c.1913, part of the famous Record series of pull-along animals.*

left: *Margarete Steiff GmbH, 1912, one of only 494 black Steiff bears to be produced for a British market that was mourning the loss of the* **Titanic.**

In 1907 Bing decided to capitalize on the craze for teddy bears. The first bears it produced bore an incredible likeness to those of Steiff in design and overall look: the mohair was of a similar density and quality, as were the colours chosen; felt pads were used on the large feet and paws; almost identical boot-button eyes were set in a very similar-shaped face; the back was humped and the arms were longer than the legs. The bears even had a metal button as an identification mark (albeit in the right ear). Steiff immediately objected, claiming its copyright had been infringed. In response Bing changed the button to a metal tag in the form of an arrow, which it continued to place in the bear's right ear. Steiff still objected. Bing's next move was to replace the arrow with a button fixed to the body of the bear beneath its left arm. After lengthy legal battles Steiff agreed that this was acceptable, as long as the word 'button' did not appear on the mark. The final solution was for Bing to identify its bears by a metal button on the right arm incised 'GBN' for Gebrüder Bing, Nürnberg.

The marked similarities between Steiff and Bing bears during this period can cause problems for experts trying to identify early teddies. There are subtle differences between the two, however, and it is these differences that experts look out for when they are challenged by a bear without an identification tag (this happens often, for tags, buttons and labels were commonly removed by cautious nannies and parents who feared they might be swallowed). Unlike Steiff, Bing often embroidered the noses of its bears with a double thread at

left: *Gebrüder Bing, c.1910. Bing used its experience of manufacturing automated toy cars to produce clockwork teddy bears such as this one.*

either end. The ears used by both companies were small, rounded and set wide apart, but Steiff ears tend to be more cupped. Further differences can be found in the length and shape of the limbs, the wrist and ankle definition, the shape of the paws and the roundness of the feet. Generally Bing was less consistent in its designs than Steiff, so that, for example, if the quality of mohair on two otherwise identical bears is different, they are more likely to have been produced by Bing.

One feature that is unique to a few Bing bears produced during a short period only is all-in-one ears. Usually ears are made from two separate pieces of plush stitched on to the head, but for these bears just one piece of material was used for both head and ears. Although it is much more difficult to shape the head using this method, Bing managed to produce delightful perfectly rounded ears.

Bing's early experience of producing tinplate and mechanical toys allowed it to excel in the production of clockwork performing bears, and today its bears are recognized as possibly the best in this field. Some of these bears were cuddly toys that could perform basic movements, such as turning their heads from side to side; others were novelty toys that were designed to walk on all fours, rollerskate or kick a football. Around 1910 Bing produced a somersaulting bear that once more landed the firm in court. Steiff objected, complaining that it was a copy of its Purzel Bär, produced in 1909. Although the Steiff bear was freestanding while the Bing acrobat hung from a wooden frame, there were enough similarities to prolong the legal battle for four years from 1911.

The company continued to grow until World War I, and by 1914 it employed 5,000 people. During the war Bing, like other manufacturers, was forced to convert its factories to production of military goods. When Ignaz Bing died in 1918 his son Stephen became director general, changing the name to Bing Werke. From 1920 the company's mark was also changed to a red button bearing the letters 'BW'.

Gebrüder Bing may have been strongly influenced by Steiff, but its actions paled into insignificance when compared with those of the Wilhelm Strunz Felt Toy Co in Allersberg and Nuremberg. As early as 1905 Strunz – quite openly and with complete disregard for the law – began to copy Steiff toys. It would buy Steiff products, take them to pieces – making careful note of the method of assembly – use the

below, top and bottom left: Pre-1919 Bing bears were marked 'GBN'.
below, top and bottom right: Bing toys were marked 'BW' after 1919.

right: *Gebrüder Bing, Jimmy,
c.1908. Ivy Tapp, who is seen in
the photograph, named her bear
Jimmy after her father, James Tapp,
who gave her the toy on her seventh
birthday, 14 February 1908.*

parts to make patterns, and then produce exact copies of the originals. (In fact the copies were less than exact, as Strunz was unwilling or unable to reproduce Steiff's quality and attention to detail.)

One of the first teddy bears Strunz copied was Steiff's rod-jointed Bär 28 PB. The poor imitations shared many characteristics with the original, including a metal button in the ear, albeit six-sided, with a label attached. Franz Steiff made every effort to persuade Strunz to withdraw the mark, but eventually he had to resort to the law to enforce the Button-In-Ear trademark. The seemingly endless arguments resulted in a compromise: on 28 October 1908 Strunz was given permission to use a paper label in the ear of its bears on condition that it was attached by a staple, not a button. Although Strunz accepted the compromise, it continued to steal ideas from Steiff.

A distinguishing feature of Strunz bears is that from 1910 they were all marked 'Präsident' (President), a reference to Teddy Roosevelt, the 'Father of the Bear'. It is almost certain that the company did not survive World War I, as there are no known postwar examples.

Some 100km (60 miles) north of Nuremberg was another German toymaking centre, this time specializing in soft toys. In Sonneberg there were dozens, if not hundreds, of small firms mass-producing cheap and cheerful products, largely for the home market. One company whose toys were a cut above the rest was Educa, founded by Eduard Crämer in 1896. Crämer, the son of a tailor, was born in 1858 in Schalkau, a small village 16km (10 miles) from Sonneberg. He attended tailoring school in Dresden, intending eventually to take over his father's business, but Schalkau had a surfeit of tailors, so Crämer was forced to look for an alternative line of work.

Fortunately help was at hand. His father-in-law, Paul Schwabacher, was a toy manufacturer in the same village, and he encouraged Crämer to design patterns for soft toys. Like Margarete Steiff, Crämer created an elephant first, although his was crudely made out of old bedcovers.

Crämer was an extremely hardworking and determined man who knew the importance of good quality and design. While other soft-toy manufacturers were producing throwaway items for fairground stands,

above: *Wilhelm Strunz Felt Toy Co., Jester Bear, c.1912, a precursor of the harlequin and clown bears of the 1920s.*

Crämer concentrated on designing well-constructed teddy bears for the export market. All his efforts were rewarded in 1906–7 when he received a huge order for 6,000 bears from a wholesaler in Sonneberg. With the proceeds from this sale he was able to build a home for himself and a factory for his business. Reinforced by his son, Hermann, and son-in-law, Heinrich Lohr, the firm flourished, although Crämer's lack of business training and capital meant that success never came easily. And, like so many toy companies, it suffered a lull in production with the outbreak of World War I.

All Educa bears were made in nine standard sizes, ranging from 20cm to 71cm (8in to 28in). They had unique heart-shaped muzzles – some with open mouths, some with felt tongues and some with somewhat comical red embroidered mouths – that made them easily identifiable (the bears carried swingtags, but no labels or buttons). The company produced many novelty designs, including brightly coloured bears, dancing and prancing bears, and a range of clown bears that would play music when their heads were gently tilted back and forth.

In addition to Germany's foremost pioneering teddy-bear makers, there were several important companies that began manufacturing before World War I but which are best known for their postwar toys. This group includes Moritz Pappe, the Hermann family, Josef Pitrmann and Schreyer & Co. (Schuco), as we shall see. And even with these the picture is still far from complete, for there were numerous smaller firms whose histories are lost to us or lie waiting to be unearthed.

opposite: *Educa, 1920s. The bears produced by Eduard Crämer can be recognized by their distinctive heart-shaped muzzles.*

BIRTH OF THE BRITISH BEAR

The third important nation in the early history of the teddy bear was Britain. The craze for bears had spread to Britain by 1908, possibly helped by the fact that the British had their own 'Teddy' in the person of King Edward VII. The first bears to appear were imported from Germany, but soon the home market began to develop, with teddies featuring in the catalogues of London-based manufacturer J.K. Farnell in 1906. This family business had been founded by John Kirby Farnell in 1840 in London's Notting Hill. The firm began as a silk merchant's, focusing on the production of small silk goods

left: *J.K. Farnell, c.1910. This bear's boot-button eyes suggest that it dates from the very first years that Farnell were making teddies.*

such as pincushions, tea cosies and penwipers. The fine needlework skills required to make such items were to stand the family in good stead in later years.

On the death of John Farnell in 1897 his son and daughter, Henry and Agnes Farnell, moved the company to a modest leased property in Acton, west London, called The Elms. It was here that they manufactured their very first soft toys and teddy bears, some of which were made out of unusual materials such as rabbit skin. They soon

right: *J.K. Farnell, 1920s. Bears by early British manufacturers like Farnell and Terry often had distinctive webbed-paw claws.*

turned to high-quality curly mohair plush, however, and began to produce first-rate bears. Like their German counterparts, early Farnell bears had pointed muzzles, long arms and legs, and humps at the top of their backs. The first Farnell bears had boot-button eyes, but the company was quick to switch to painted glass eyes. The most distinguishing feature of a Farnell bear, however, and one that is specific to British teddies, was its webbed paws: the stitches that formed the claws were linked on the paws to produce a web effect. Such details can prove vital when trying to identify an early bear, as the labelling of the initial Farnells was highly erratic – the very first bears were often unmarked, although examples with webbed-paw claws have been found.

During World War I Farnell produced fully jointed miniature bears made out of traditional golden mohair as well as the patriotic colours red, white and blue. They were given as good-luck charms to soldiers on their way to the Front by their sweethearts. Some must have worked their magic, as survivors have been found unscathed in uniform pockets more than seventy years later (the bears were made with upturned faces so that they could peer out of a breast pocket). The most famous collection of soldier bears to have emerged in recent years belonged to the twins David and Guy Campbell, born 18 January 1910. During term-time the boys attended Eton College in Berkshire, England, but they spent most of their holidays with their grandmother, Mrs Rosabelle Rawlins, at her Elizabethan manor house in Dorset. Here they were told of the heroic exploits of their soldier ancestors, who had been involved in some of the most famous events of the Victorian era, including the disastrous Charge of the

Light Brigade (1854) and the failed relief of General Gordon at Khartoum (1885).

The boys were given soldier bears by their grandmother. Usually they received one or two at a time, but one Christmas she bought them fifty. They began to use the bears to re-enact some of the adventures they had been told about, as well as events from further back in history, great sporting triumphs and scenes from bloodcurdling novels. They also began to build props, including a castle and some cottages, an Elizabethan galleon and a pirate ship, and a stagecoach for scenes from the Wild West as well as for the adventures of the highwayman Dick Turpin. Many of the bears were named after friends, relatives or characters from history, and some were dressed in homemade tunics made from scraps of old uniforms and military ribbons. The more bears the boys were given, the bigger and more intricate their re-creations became.

Like all collectors, each of the boys had their own favourite bear. David's was called Grubby, and Guy's was Young. When the twins grew up they both joined the army, taking their bears with them to the battles of World War II. Both men received the Military Cross for their bravery in action, honours that they shared with their bears. The twins and their bears remained inseparable after the war until David and Guy died within two years of each other, in the early 1990s. Then Grubby MC and Young MC found a new home at the Puppenhausmuseum in Basel, Switzerland, and the remaining 396 Farnell soldier bears in the Campbell collection were sold at auction in May 1999.

A British firm with a very similar history to J.K. Farnell's was W.J. Terry, a skin merchant's founded by

William J. Terry in 1890. Terry, too, began producing soft toys covered with real fur at the beginning of the twentieth century. By 1909, after the success of a toy dog called Terry'er based on King Edward VII's dog Caesar, the company was in a position to open a large factory at 25 Middleton Road, Hackney, London. In 1913 W.J. Terry moved to Lavender Grove, also in Hackney, and continued to develop the Terry'er Toy range, introducing, among various animals, mohair plush teddy bears.

above: J.K. Farnell, soldier bear, 1914–18, one of the bears owned by the Campbell twins.

Terry bears embraced the overall look of the Farnell, and the two have often been confused. The former have long silky mohair plush and a rather straight body with a pronounced hump. Like Farnell, Terry favoured large glass eyes with painted backs rather than boot buttons. It also adopted the Farnell webbed-paw claws.

On the death of William Terry in 1924 his son, Frederick, struggled to continue the business. Like many such companies, however, it was deeply affected by the worldwide Depression in the 1930s, and production had ceased by World War II.

Harwin & Co. Ltd, another producer of top-quality teddy bears, had an even briefer existence. Many experts are of the opinion that it, too, was influenced by Farnell, but its sales manager, Fred Taylor, had previously worked for Steiff, and this undoubtedly had an impact on

Harwin's designs. The north London company was founded by G.W. Harwin in 1914, possibly in response to the import ban on German goods after the declaration of World War I. British firms enjoyed a monopoly in the home market and the overseas colonies as a result. Also, at the beginning of the war, the plush manufacturers of Yorkshire were unable to sell to Germany and so were keen to find new buyers for their materials. Later they ran out of raw materials, too, and switched to producing cruder goods for the war effort.

Harwin's early production focused mainly on felt dolls, which is why its most memorable and famous line of bears was dressed in the finest felt clothes, designed by the founder's daughter, Dorothy. Ally Bears wore the uniforms of World War I soldiers and sailors in the Allied forces, and those of Red Cross nurses. Although they were highly successful, today Ally Bears are very rare. One explanation for this is that they accompanied their owners to the Front and, like so many of their owners, never returned.

Harwin & Co. Ltd was also responsible for a Scottish bear in full Highland regalia, part of the Eyes Right range (the name is a reference to the bears' googly eyes). It is also thought to have made mascots for the first nonstop transatlantic flight, on 14 June 1919, when John William Alcock and Arthur Whitten Brown flew a Vickers-Vimy biplane from Newfoundland to Ireland in 16 hours and 27 minutes. Production of such high-quality dressed bears was expensive, however, and Harwin & Co. Ltd was forced to close in the early 1930s.

One early British manufacturer that has survived the vicissitudes of the twentieth

right: *Humphrey, 1910s. This bear's long straight body, wide-set ears and large staring eyes all suggest that it is an early example by W.J. Terry.*

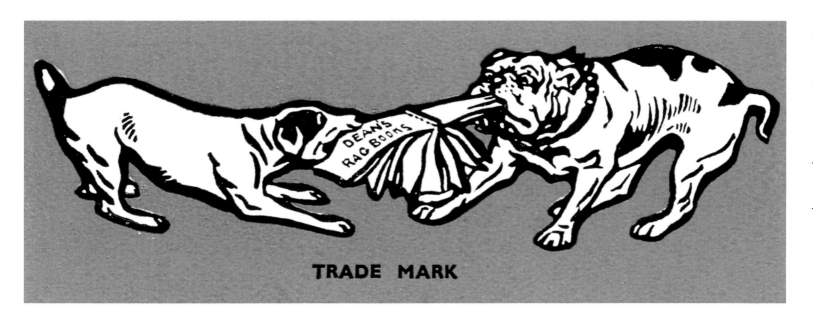

TRADE MARK

century to this day is Dean's Rag Book Co. Ltd, which was founded in 1903 by Henry Samuel Dean just off London's Fleet Street. The company specialized in indestructible rag books 'for children who wear their food and eat their clothes', an attitude symbolized in its trademark depicting two dogs fighting over a rag book. It was a subsidiary of Dean & Son Ltd, a printing and publishing firm established in the eighteenth century that was one of the first houses to design and produce entertaining books for children. Whether an ABC or an edition of Perrault's fairy tales, a Dean & Son book would contain an abundance of illustrations, emphasizing that learning should be a pleasure rather than a chore. During the nineteenth century its products became increasingly recreational, with three-dimensional books introduced in the 1840s, followed by colouring books in the 1870s.

In 1908 the Dean's Rag Book Co. produced a printed-cloth teddy bear as part of its Knockabout Toys series. The cotton bear had to be cut out from a printed

sheet and assembled at home. In the same year it also issued a teddy-bear rag book. In 1912 the company moved to Elephant & Castle in southeast London, and three years later it produced its first plush mohair teddy bear. Launched under the Kuddlemee brand name, he had pointed ears and long jointed limbs. Production was limited during World War I (although one printed patriotic teddy called The Bear of Russia, Germany's Crusher was issued) and was further interrupted by a fire in 1916, which destroyed many early samples.

Another manufacturer to introduce teddy bears in 1915 was The Chad Valley Co. Ltd. This firm had begun life as a bookbinder and printer some ninety-five years earlier, founded in Birmingham by Anthony Bunn Johnson. His sons, Joseph and Alfred, set up their own stationery firm, Messrs Johnson Bros., in 1860, also in Birmingham. By 1889 Joseph's son, Alfred J. Johnson, had joined the family business, and eight years later father and son moved to a new factory based in the nearby village of

above: *Dean's famous trademark of a terrier and a bulldog fighting over a rag book was designed in 1903 by the artist Stanley Berkeley.*

right: *The Chad Valley Co. Ltd, 1920s. This bear is stuffed with cork chippings, perhaps indicating a lack of materials following World War I.*

above: *Chiltern Toy Works, Master Teddy, c.1915, two of the five different sizes of this model available.*

right: *Harwin & Co. Ltd, Eyes Right, 1914–18, a googly-eyed bear intended to raise the morale of the Scottish regiments during World War I.*

right: *Rare Einco, c.1920s. Without the chest tag it would be easy to mistake this bear for a Farnell.*

German imports during World War I. This ban undoubtedly prompted the introduction of soft toys to its range, with the first teddy bears making their appearance in 1915. Some of these wartime bears were filled with cork chippings, perhaps owing to a lack of excelsior. The problem must have been solved, however, because in 1916 the company patented a stuffing machine for soft toys.

Chad Valley continued to make teddy bears throughout the war years, and by 1920 it had opened a separate premises for soft toys in Welling, Shropshire. Initially called the Wrekin Toy Works, it was later named the Chad Valley Co. Ltd. The company's printworks remained at Harborne Village Institute.

Many existing toy companies took advantage of the British ban on German imports during World War I to expand into the teddy-bear market. One such firm was the British United Toy Manufacturing Co. Ltd, founded as James S. Renvoize Ltd in 1894 to produce lead toy soldiers. It added teddy bears and other soft toys to its range in 1911, and witnessed a boom in production during the war. In 1914 it introduced Coaster Toys, including a teddy bear on wheels that was remarkably similar to Steiff's Record Teddy. In the same year the company adopted the tradename Omega, although it was not officially registered until 1929.

One of the reasons the war had such an enormous effect on the teddy-bear industry was that the British and German markets were closely linked. Chiltern Toys, for example, was founded in Germany in 1881 as a toy export

Harborne. It was here that the Chad Valley trademark was born, inspired by the Chad stream that ran through Harborne. By 1900 the product range had been extended to include cardboard games. On the death of his father in 1904 Alfred J. Johnson led the company as chairman and managing director, supported by his family, his brothers Arthur and Henry and brother-in-law William Riley.

Chad Valley began increasingly to concentrate on toys, and production grew steadily, helped by the ban on

company by brothers Josef and Gabriel Eisenmann. Josef was based in London, at 45 Whitecross Street, while Gabriel stayed in Fürth in Bavaria. Around 1900 German-born Leon Rees joined Josef Eisenmann as a business partner, leaving his homeland to settle in Britain. This partnership was strengthened by Leon's marriage to Josef's daughter. Eisenmann & Co. Ltd is thought to have introduced teddy bears from Germany to Britain, and certainly had an influence on J.K. Farnell's bears. In 1908 Eisenmann opened the Chiltern Works, a toy factory based in Chesham, Buckinghamshire, concentrating on doll production. As with so many British firms, it was the onset of war that led it to turn to teddy-bear making, when it launched Master Teddy in 1915. This curious-looking chap – he is often referred to today, with wry understatement, as 'not the most handsome of bears' – was based on a character in *The Teddy Tail League*, a cartoon published in the *Daily Mail*, and inherited his wide-set googly eyes. Despite his lack of good looks, Master Teddy is highly collectable today, particularly if he is still dressed in his pink checked shirt, blue felt trousers and braces. Other teddies produced by Eisenmann & Co. Ltd (which often traded under the name 'Einco') had webbed-paw claws, and are often mistaken for Farnell bears today.

Also rather odd-looking are the bears produced by Steevans Manufacturing Co. Ltd. Little is known about this British company, which flourished from around 1910 to the early 1920s. At least two labelled teddies have been recorded to date, and there are other unmarked toys that are stongly suspected of being Steevans bears. They are often fairly crudely designed, but their rarity makes them highly collectable today.

The years 1904 to 1919 were perhaps the most crucial in the history of the teddy. The perfected designs of Richard Steiff, which were taken up by companies in Germany, the USA and Britain, fuelled an unprecedented demand for the bears. And, unlike so many fads for other 'must-have' toys, this craze did not die out. So, when World War I cut off the traditional sources for teddies in Germany, established manufacturers in Britain seized the opportunity to develop their own lines, while new companies sprange up to join them, providing active competition into the 1920s.

below: *Steevans Manufacturing Co. Ltd, 1910s, rose-coloured, with musical chimes that play when the bear is rocked.*

The Bear at War

With the outbreak of World War I production almost came to a halt across continental Europe, as factory workers and owners were called up for military service and buildings were commandeered for the war effort. Many British firms produced patriotic mascots, sometimes dressed in the uniforms of the Allied forces. Teddy bears gave comfort to those serving on the Western Front, and to the millions of children left fatherless after the war. During World War II raw materials were rationed, and commercially produced teddies often had shorter necks, limbs and muzzles in order to save on fabric. Teddy bears helped to reassure children terrified by bombing and the effects of war, including the many thousands who were evacuated from the cities.

❶ *Many European teddy-bear manufacturers contributed to the war effort by producing soldier bears during World War I. Some, such as J.K. Farnell, made miniature teddies that could be carried in a uniform pocket. Others made larger bears that travelled in their owner's knapsack. Harwin & Co.'s series of bears wearing Allied uniforms, known as Ally Bears, were dressed in felt with painstaking attention to detail. Some were taken to the Front, but, at 30cm (12 in) tall, others such as this British lieutenant were left behind as keepsakes for sweethearts or children.*

❷ *During World War II, everybody in Britain was issued with a gas mask, which they had to carry with them at all times. Children were often frightened by such an ugly reminder of the dangers they faced and to reassure them special cases were made, including this example decorated with a mohair teddy bear made by Farnell and wearing felt clothes. This measure may also have helped to reduce the number of instances where children forgot their masks, as many would be reluctant to leave a teddy bear in peril.*

❸ Many children were evacuated to the country during World War II. Although they were very limited in the amount of luggage they could take with them, their teddy bears were looked upon as a necessity rather than a luxury. The toys also gave comfort to those children who remained in the cities during wartime, including this group who were photographed on 15 September 1940 sitting outside their bombed homes in the morning after an air raid on London.

❹ Soldier bears were again popular during World War II. Illustrated here is Sneezy, a miniature Chad Valley teddy bear, shown with a photograph of his original owner, Ted Able. Sneezy was given to Ted by his mother as a lucky keepsake on his departure to the overseas conflict in 1941. The charm worked, and Ted and Sneezy returned safely after the war. Sneezy remained in Norfolk on his owner's bedside table until 1991, when Ted died aged 81 years.

❺ The raw materials needed to make teddy bears, including mohair plush and kapok stuffing, were in limited supply during wartime. Those manufacturers who continued production sought cheap, plentiful alternatives such as cotton plush. Sheepskin was another option, and white sheepskin teddies were traditionally matched with black leather paw pads, as in this example by J.K. Farnell from the late 1940s.

chapter 3

THE ROARING BEAR

(1920–1949)

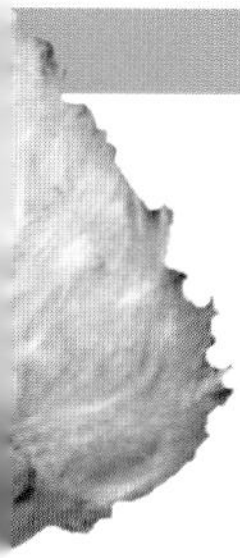

In the years following World War I, with many in Britain and abroad reluctant to buy German goods, and with Germany struggling to pay crippling reparations, the British teddy-bear industry flourished. By 1921 J.K. Farnell had outgrown its modest Acton home, The Elms, so a new factory was built next door. This addition was known as the Alpha Works and was managed by Agnes Farnell. Staff numbers were increased to cope with the orders that were flooding in.

right: Farnell bears dating from the 1920s, shown with Jemima Puddle-Duck from its Beatrix Potter range.

Among the new recruits was H.C. Janisch, who was head of sales throughout the 1920s, before becoming a founding member of a rival company, Merrythought.

Aided by the imaginative designer Sybil Kemp, J.K. Farnell continued to produce top-quality soft toys. Among these were the famous Alpha Bears, a range that showed striking similarities to Richard Steiff's classic teddy bear of 1905. When Alpha Bears were first launched in the early 1920s they had golden or silver/white mohair plush, vertically stitched oblong noses, long arms, sturdy thighs, narrow ankles and large oval feet.

The world's most famous Alpha Bear was purchased in 1921, reportedly from Harrods in London, by the writer A.A. Milne as a present for his son, Christopher Robin, on his first birthday. In 1924 Milne published a book of children's poems entitled *When We Were Very Young* and illustrated by E.H. Shepard, who worked for *Punch* magazine. The collection included the poem 'Teddy Bear', describing a little bear with a weight problem. This was the first, unofficial, appearance of Pooh; he was properly launched in a story written for the Christmas Eve issue of the *Evening News* in 1925. This went on to form the first chapter of *Winnie the Pooh* (1926), a collection of short stories about Christopher Robin and his nursery toys. The book was an enormous success and was followed in 1928 by *The House at Pooh Corner*. The original Farnell teddy, which was always known as Edward Bear by Christopher Robin, now resides at the New York Public Library, along with his soft toy friends Piglet, Eeyore, Tigger, Kanga and Roo.

Although J.K Farnell had been advertising Alpha Bears since the early 1920s, it did not register the Alpha trademark until 1925. All bears before that date were labelled with paper tags printed with the words 'Alpha Make'. Post-1925 products carried a white cloth label embroidered in blue which read: 'Farnell Alpha Toys Made in England' or 'A Farnell Alpha Toy Made in England'.

Throughout the 1920s and 1930s J.K. Farnell continued to expand its range. Since February 1920, when the Teddy Toy Co. had patented its Softanlite kapok stuffing, British manufacturers had been using the light silky fibres that grow on the seedpods of the *Bombax ceiba* tree of India and Malaysia and the *Ceiba pentandra* tree of tropical America. Farnell was no exception, and from the mid-1920s most of its bears were at least part-stuffed with kapok, making them lighter, softer and more hygienic. Among the other innovations seen during this period was the introduction around 1926 of dual mohair plush, where the tips of the bear's pale coat were brushed with a darker dye (Steiff launched its dual mohair plush teddies in the same year). Then, in March 1929, came the arrival of its Silkalite bear, whose coat was made from artificial-silk plush woven from a cellulose-based fibre. The year 1929 was a momentous one for J.K. Farnell. On 25 January its co-founder, Agnes Farnell died. She had been involved in toy design since the company's beginnings. Later that year, however, Farnell launched itself on the international stage, opening showrooms in New York and Paris and arranging distribution of its products throughout Canada and the USA.

The timing was far from auspicious, for the year 1929 proved a disastrous one generally: October brought the Wall Street Crash, and its reverberations triggered the subsequent worldwide Depression. Understandably, in this

climate there was less demand for luxury toys. Farnell found that its Alpha Toys were constantly being undercut by European imports. In response in 1931 it introduced cheaper Unicorn Soft Toys, which were sold alongside the quality range. Among these more affordable toys was Cuddle Bear, available in four different sizes and colours.

The Unicorn range was to be short lived, however, for in 1934 the Acton factory and entire stock was

above: A.A. Milne with his son Christopher Robin and Edward Bear.

above: *J.K. Farnell, Alpha Bear, 1920s. The teddy's cloth label is clearly visible on the pad of its left foot.*

destroyed by fire. Although the ever-popular Alpha Bear rose from the ashes, Cuddle Bear and his bargain-priced friends did not survive. In their place came new factory lines, including the lambswool plush Che-Kee and the Alpac range. The latter was a series of toys for babies using plush made from the wool of the alpaca llama, and included pink, white, blue and gold teddy bears. Among the novelty toys from this period were the Coronation Bear in red, white and blue, made for the crowning of George VI in 1937 (following the abdication of his brother, Edward VIII), and a range of musical bears using movements manufactured by the Swiss company Thorens.

Disaster struck again in 1940 when the Farnell factory was once more destroyed, this time during the Blitz. Although the company recovered from the war, it was an uphill struggle as, like so many British soft-toy companies, it suffered heavily from a shortage of materials (bears dating from this period tend to have shortened muzzles and stubby limbs to economize on plush). The company's remaining co-founder, Henry Kirby Farnell, died in 1944. As if signalling a new era, in the following year a new label was introduced. Printed in red, white and blue, the words 'Farnell Alpha Hygienic Soft Toy' were written in a shield shape above 'Made in England'.

One company whose bears are often mistaken for those of Farnell is Invicta Toys Ltd. The confusion is hardly surprising, as Invicta was founded in 1935 by G.E. Beer and T.W. Wright, previously a director and a sales representative respectively at Farnell. This crossfertilization of designs and manufacture methods through the movement of employees happened throughout the soft-toy industry and greatly enriched the product, although it makes it much more difficult to identify the source of unlabelled teddy bears.

Invicta's London-based factory produced a large range of wheeled and traditional teddy bears and soft toys, including ones named Teddy, Sammy and Grizzlie. During World War II soft-toy production was suspended as the factory was required to produce military equipment, including weapons. The company made a healthy recovery after the war, though, thriving until G.E. Beer retired in 1954, when trading ceased.

Since 1915 teddy-bear cartoons had been featuring in British newspapers, fanning the flames of the toy's popularity. In 1920 the editor of the *Daily Express*, R.D. Blumenfeld, was instructed by the newspaper's owner,

left: *J.K. Farnell, Dual Plush Alpha Bear, 1920s. The teddy's long, curly golden mohair is tipped with brown.*

Lord Beaverbrook, to find and launch a comicstrip that would outstrip those of its competitors. Blumenfeld commissioned Mary Tourtel, the wife of his night-news editor and a well-established illustrator of children's books. The result was Rupert, a white bear with checked trousers and scarf. He first appeared in the *Daily Express* on 8 November 1920 in a story called 'The Adventures of a Little Lost Bear', and the tale unfolded day by day in the

form of a picture accompanied by a set of rhymes. One by one, Rupert's band of friends in Nutwood village were introduced, including Bill Badger, Algy Pug, Edward Trunk and Podgy Pig.

In 1935, the year of the first Rupert annual, illhealth forced Mary Tourtel to retire. A replacement artist was found in Alfred Bestall, who continued the strip until 1965. By this time the spin-offs and merchandising opportunities had snowballed, and a whole group of artists and writers were brought in to continue the adventures of Rupert Bear, a situation that endures today.

Although Dean's Rag Book Co. had made its first teddy bears in 1915, dolls continued to form the bulk of its production. In 1922 it registered the tradename A1 Toys for a range that included slender mohair plush bears, stuffed with wood-wool and with either a squeaker or a growler voicebox; they also had a wide variety of labels and swingtags throughout production. As well as its traditional lines, in the 1920s Dean's produced novelty toys such as the Evripoze Bears, whose patented joints meant they could hold their arms and legs in various positions, and bears with strikingly coloured fur and eyes.

Teddy-bear production at Dean's increased considerably during the 1930s. In common with many British manufacturers, the firm began to alter the shape of the bear subtly during this period, shortening the arms, legs and body to give a much stockier shape. It also began to show a preference for artificial-silk plush, using it for all the bears in the 1935 catalogue, perhaps because of its comparative cheapness, or maybe because it could easily be dyed one of the

right: J.K. Farnell, 1930s. The paw pads on this bear are made from Rexine, an imitation leather.

many colours that were fashionable at the time (although coloured bears were generally rejected when they were first introduced by Steiff in 1908, they were now highly sought after). Traditional mohair plush was not jettisoned, though, as it reappeared the next year.

In 1937 the company moved to a new factory in Merton, in southwest London. There it continued to make soft toys until the outbreak of World War II, when it switched production to military supplies such as life jackets and Bren-gun covers. Like many toy manufacturers, Dean's found the period immediately after the war particularly difficult – people were more concerned with rebuilding their homes and their lives than with buying teddy bears – and it was not until 1949 that it issued a new catalogue.

The company often drew on current events for inspiration, and in that year it produced a mother polar bear, Ivy, with a cub, to celebrate the birth of Brumas, the first polar bear ever to be born at London Zoo. A.A. Milne, too, in his introduction to *Winnie the Pooh*, paid homage to Pooh's arctic neighbours:

'The nicest people go straight to the animal they love the most, and stay there. So when Christopher Robin goes to the Zoo, he goes to where the Polar Bears are, and he whispers something to the third keeper from the left, and doors are unlocked, and we wander through dark passages and up steep stairs until at last we come to the special cage, and the cage is opened, and out trots something brown and furry [Winnie], and with a happy cry of "Oh, Bear!" Christopher Robin rushes into its arms.'

One of the most successful teddy-bear manufacturers of the interwar period was The Chad Valley Co. Ltd,

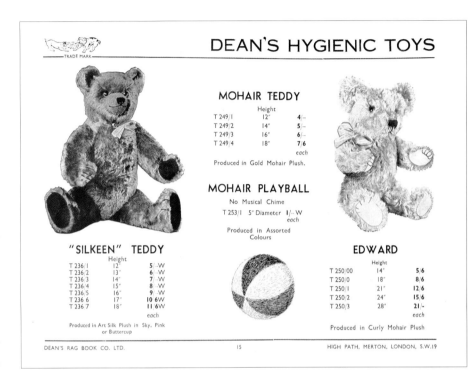

which managed by careful expansion to create a range of bears for all tastes and pockets. In 1923 it began to use kapok stuffing in its soft toys, which it marketed under the Aerolite trademark – between 1923 and 1926 toys that contained the new stuffing were presented with a button marked 'Aerolite'. In fact, all Chad Valley bears produced in the 1920s and 1930s were identified by a maker's button or printed label, or both. Buttons were placed in the right ears of some teddy bears, but Steiff must have complained, as later examples have buttons attached to the chest, chin or back.

In 1923 Chad Valley bought Isaacs & Co., a Birmingham manufacturer that specialized in soft 'Isa' toys with hidden springs in their legs (when the toys were patted they would bounce gently up and down). Five years later the Harborne factory was extended to

above: Among the toys advertised in this Dean's catalogue from the 1930s is a range of teddy bears made from Silkeen, an artificial silk plush.

accommodate an increase in production. The company was further enlarged in 1931 when it took over Peacock & Co. Ltd, a London firm established in 1853 that produced wooden kindergarten toys and games such as educational maps, puzzles, and building and alphabet blocks. Chad Valley switched the manufacture of these toys to a new factory in Clerkenwell, London, while making teddy bears under the Peacock label at the Harborne works. The overall look of the Peacock bears was very similar to that of the Chad Valley Magna Series; in particular, both had narrow rectangular and horizontally stitched noses. The Peacock range of bears was discontinued after World War II.

During the 1920s and 1930s Chad Valley's teddies, like most British bears, were changing shape and becoming cuddlier. Arms and legs were gradually shortened, feet became smaller and the hump at the top of the back became far less prominent. Chad Valley noses were particularly distinctive. In the 1920s they tended to be triangular, made up of vertical stitches and completed by a row of horizontal stitches along the top. The Magna Series bears of the 1930s had rectangular noses, but other lines had oval noses that were thickly bound and vertically stitched. The ears were also larger and flatter than those on other makes of bear.

Choosing a Chad Valley bear was no simple matter in the 1930s: customers could pick from fourteen different sizes and select either kapok or wood-wool stuffing – or both; the quality and texture of mohair plush could be varied, or the bear could be made from artificial-silk plush; and a number of colours were available other than the traditional browns and golden hues (blue was a

opposite: A group of teddy bears made by Chad Valley and dating from the 1920s to the 1950s.

particularly popular colour, a change from 1908 when Steiff's blue Elliot had been cruelly spurned). One of the most popular lines was Cubby Bear, blessed with two complementary brown tones of alpaca plush. With his high forehead, short arms and long body he was a soft and gentle bear that remained popular into the 1950s.

In 1938 Chad Valley was appointed toymaker to Queen Elizabeth, the consort of George VI. This royal warrant is useful when trying to date Chad Valley bears: from 1938 to 1953 they wore a label marked 'By Appointment Toymakers to Her Majesty the Queen'; after the coronation of Elizabeth II the labels read 'By Appointment Toy Makers to H.M. Queen Elizabeth The Queen Mother'.

Unlike many other toymakers, Chad Valley did not cease production of soft toys altogether during World War II, although the Wrekin Toy Works in Wellington, Shropshire, was turned over to the manufacture of children's clothes. Rigorous cuts had to be made to its teddies, however: bears dating from this period tend to be thinner and with shorter limbs than their predecessors, as stuffing was at a premium. Mohair plush was also scarce, so the company experimented with other materials; white sheepskin bears with black leather pads were a particularly stylish innovation.

Chad Valley continued to blossom after the war, and during the next two decades the firm purchased a further six companies. The first of these, in 1946, was A.S. Cartwright of Birmingham, which produced aluminium wares. It was followed swiftly by Waterloo Works, Wellington, manufacturers of rubber goods.

By the 1930s the first generation of teddy-bear owners had grown up and were beginning to feel nostalgic about their old toys. This feeling was captured by

above: *Chad Valley Co. Ltd, 1930s, a particularly unusual teddy from a company known for their coloured bears.*

Dodie Smith, the British author and dramatist best known for *101 Dalmatians*, in her play *Dear Octopus*, which debuted in London's West End in the 1930s. In the following extract Cynthia, the prodigal daughter, returns to her family home and, going into the nursery, finds a child called Scrap. There is also a teddy bear:

CYNTHIA   Is that a teddy bear? Why, it's Symp!
SCRAP   Symp?
CYNTHIA   We call him that because he was extra

sympathetic. We used to hug him whenever we were miserable, when we were in disgrace or rabbits died or when nobody understood us.
SCRAP   Did Mummy hug him?
CYNTHIA   We all did. It went on 'til we were quite big. Hello, Symp, my lad, how did you lose that arm?
SCRAP   Is he still sympathetic?
CYNTHIA   He looks it to me. His fur used to get sopping wet with tears. Oh, comfortable Symp! He must be over thirty years old.

It was during this era of nostalgia that one of the most prestigious British soft-toy manufacturers took to the field, surprisingly late in the day. Since its founding in 1930, however, Merrythought has been producing soft toys with a hint of magic. The story of Merrythought actually begins some eleven years earlier, when, in 1919, W.G. Holmes and G.H. Laxton opened a small spinning mill in Yorkshire to produced mohair yarn from imported raw materials. The introduction of cheaper synthetic fibres such as artificial silk in the late 1920s created competition for those in the mohair-producing industry, and many suppliers suffered as a result. One company that experienced a substantial loss of business was the mohair plush weaver Tyson Hall & Co. Ltd, which was based in Bakersfield, Yorkshire, and was a customer of Holmes and Laxton. Facing the loss of a significant client, Holmes and Laxton bought Tyson Hall & Co. Ltd; they then had to find a way to put the mohair plush to good use.

They decided to start manufacturing soft toys, and in 1930 they founded Merrythought Ltd. The reason for this unusual name is not known. 'Merrythought' is an Old English word for a wishbone (the company's trademark), and perhaps they thought that such a happy-sounding word combined with a traditional symbol of good luck made an irresistible combination. Next they had to hire key members of staff, and luckily for them two of the most experienced men in the industry were ready to move jobs. C.J. Rendle, head of toy production at Chad Valley, and A.C. Janisch, head of sales at J.K. Farnell, both joined as directors of the new company. Property was rented from the Coalbrookdale Co. in what is now Ironbridge, Shropshire, and so began the production of Merrythought toys.

As often happens when senior managers move from one company to another, staff from both Chad Valley and J.K. Farnell followed Rendle and Janisch to Merrythought. Perhaps the most important of these was Florence Atwood, an impressive individual with exceptional talent and creativity. Born a deaf-mute, Florence studied design at the Deaf and Dumb School in Manchester. It was here that she was introduced to Rendle, whose daughter attended the same school.

Florence joined Merrythought in 1930 and in that year became solely responsible for designing the entire collection of thirty-two soft toys presented in the first catalogue in 1931. She not only devised original lines, such as the much-loved Greyfriars Bobby (based on the famous Skye terrier, who from 1858 to his own death in 1872 kept watch over his master's grave), but also transformed famous storybook and comic characters into extremely popular soft toys, including MGM's Tom and Jerry, G.E. Studdy's Bonzo and Cloe Preston's Dinkie the Dog. It was also in this 1931 catalogue that Merrythought proudly introduced its first two teddies: Magnet Bear and Merrythought Bear.

The first Merrythought bears were made from golden mohair plush. Like many other British bears produced during the 1930s, they had short sturdy legs and rounded arms ending in spoon-shaped paws. Magnet Bear had an appealing babyish look, with his fluffy coat, high forehead and plump little body stuffed with kapok. The Merrythought line, which later became known as the M line, was more traditional looking. Like the Chad Valley bears of the same period, they had large flat ears and a shaved muzzle, while their webbed paws were pure J.K. Farnell. The Merrythought nose – made up of vertical

left: Merrythought Ltd, early 1930s. The button in the ear of this bear reveals that it is from the first few years of production.

left: *Chiltern Toys, Hugmee, 1920s, showing the distinctive raised stitches at each side of the bear's nose.*

above: *Merrythought Ltd, Dutch Teddy, c.1938. This bear's corduroy trousers are reminiscent of those worn by Dutchmen.*

right: *Merrythought Ltd, Clown Bear, 1930s, a harlequin-style teddy in three colours of mohair plush.*

stitches and finishing with a dropped stitch at each end, giving the effect of laughter lines – was original, however, and sat above a Y-shaped mouth. Like Chad Valley, and of course Steiff, Merrythought identified its early bears by attaching a celluloid-covered pewter button to one of the ears. The button was printed with 'Hygienic Merrythought Toys' and the trademark wishbone. These were soon replaced, however, by woven cloth labels reading 'Merrythought Hygienic Toys Made in England', which were attached to the right foot. This promotion of hygiene was to continue throughout the 1930s and 1940s in Britain, culminating in the washable bears of Wendy Boston in the 1950s.

Perhaps the most successful of the teddy bears produced by Merrythought in 1931 was Bingie, a sitting bear cub. With his big floppy ears lined with artificial-silk plush, large head with a long brow, soft body covered in shaggy mohair plush, and short arms and legs leading to outsized feet, he had the endearing features of a baby animal and was immediately taken to people's hearts. The line, which ran from 1931 to 1938, was expanded so that eventually Merrythought was producing Bingies in seven different sizes, including two tiny bears (known as Baby Bingies) intended for the youngest of customers. In 1933 the company introduced a series of full-size Bingies dressed in the felt outfits of, among others, a boy, a girl, a sailor and a guardsman. The bears had mohair plush on their heads and the backs of their paws, but beneath their clothes their bodies were made of brushed cotton.

The first Merrythought catalogue was warmly received by industry and public alike, and soon the company had to grow to meet the demand for its toys.

opposite: Chiltern Toys, Hugmee, 1940s, with shortened muzzle in response to World War II rationing.

Florence Atwood was appointed chief designer (a position she held until her death in 1949) and in 1932 her second catalogue – filled with a huge variety of wonderful wild, domestic, wheeled and dressed animals – illustrated the degree of her extraordinary talent. Her designs, many of which are still in production today, ensured that Merrythought quickly became one of the leading soft-toy manufacturers in the world.

In 1939 the Coalbrookdale factory was taken over by the British Admiralty, which produced essential maps there throughout World War II. Merrythought moved to nearby Wellington, where it switched manufacture from soft toys to practical fabric items for the government, including gasmask bags, helmet linings and military chevrons.

Merrythought was able to resume production at the Coalbrookdale factory in March 1946. Disaster struck later that year, however, when the nearby River Severn flooded, destroying a large proportion of the company's archive and materials. Things might have gone very badly indeed had it not been for the actions of B. Trayton Holmes, son of one of the co-founders. He joined Merrythought in 1949 and – by investing in new equipment, erecting a design studio and showroom and improving the original factory building – set the firm back on its feet.

Though founded a decade earlier, in 1920, H.G. Stone & Co. was akin to Merrythought in having close personnel links with J.K. Farnell. Harry Stone was an ex-employee who joined forces with Leon Rees – who had inherited the Chiltern Works in Chesham from his father-in-law, Josef Eisenmann, the previous year – to form a new soft-toy company. In 1921 they opened a second factory in Tottenham, north London. Stone was responsible for design and manufacture, while Rees took care of marketing. One of the first teddies they produced together was Baby Bruin, a bear cub that, with his fluffy coat and outstretched arms, was just begging to be loved. The first range of toys to be sold under the Chiltern Toys label was launched in 1923 (although the name was not officially registered until the following year) and included the hugely successful Hugmee bears. These rather square-faced but broadly smiling teddies had long shaved muzzles. As with Merrythought's bears, the nose embroidery was distinctive: the outer stitches on each side of a Chiltern rectangular nose extended upwards towards the eyes. The head was stuffed with woodwool, while the trunk, arms and legs were filled with kapok. If the bear was fitted with a squeaker – and most were – this was protected by woodwool. Like most British bears of the period, Hugmees had chunky thighs and slim ankles, although their feet were unusually large. Their arms were long and curved, ending in spoon-shaped paws.

By the end of the 1920s H.G. Stone & Co. was one of Britain's leading manufacturers of high-quality teddy bears and soft toys. It had always been careful to use the finest mohair plush on its toys, but this did not stop it from introducing in 1929 one of the first artificial-silk plush bears on the market. Known as Silky Teddy, it too proved remarkably popular with a public hungry for new materials.

Luckier than most soft-toy companies, H.G. Stone & Co. was able to continue work throughout World War II at its London factory, although production was halted at the Chesham works. Among the toys dating from this period were a number of patriotic bears, including one dressed in the uniform of a Home Guard sergeant. Hugmees were also made,

although the design was altered slightly in response to a shortage of materials (1940s Hugmees can be recognized by their shorter muzzles). After the war, in anticipation of a boom in the market, the company relocated to Pontypool, Wales, opening a school to train the local workforce in soft-toy manufacture in 1946, before moving full-scale production there the following year.

A major rival of Merrythought and H.G. Stone & Co. – indeed, one of the world's largest and most successful toy manufacturers in the mid-twentieth century – was Lines Bros. Ltd. This family business began in the 1870s when two brothers, George and Joseph Lines, formed G. & J. Lines Ltd, a London firm that focused primarily on the production of wooden toys such as rocking horses. Upon Joseph's retirement George

right: *Pedigree Soft Toys Ltd, late 1950s. This bear is made of second-rate materials, but still seems to have been enthusiastically loved.*

continued the business with the help of his sons. Production was interrupted when war was declared in 1914 and George's sons had to leave for the trenches. On return from service, three of his sons – William, Arthur and Walter – decided to set up their own company, Lines Bros. Ltd, while the eldest son remained with his father. The new company's very distinctive tradename, Tri-ang Toys, was illustrated by a triangle, each side representing one of the three inseparable brothers. In 1924 the firm moved to a state-of-the-art factory in Merton, southwest London, where the brothers continued to produce the same sort of items as their father. In 1931 Lines Bros. Ltd registered a range of prams it was producing under the trademark Pedigree. Six years later it launched its first catalogue of Pedigree Soft Toys, in which teddy bears featured, and soon it was producing goods in factories around the world, including Australia, New Zealand, Canada and South Africa.

The design and manufacture of Pedigree teddy bears was less good than those of many of their competitors, but they were competitively priced – which was very important during the 1930s and 1940s, when the Depression was followed by war – and so found favour with wholesale buyers. Typically they were cheerful and straightforward-looking bears, with very round heads, short muzzles, straight arms and legs, and small round velvet-padded feet. At the time the toys were remarkably successful – in fact in 1946 Pedigree opened a second factory in Belfast, Northern Ireland. The bears have not become prized collectors' items, however, which must be a result of their inferior quality and ready availability.

One of the remarkable aspects of the teddy-bear industry during the first half of the twentieth century is

the large number of influential women designers, managers and owners at a time when women over thirty had only just gained the vote (in 1918; those under thirty would have to wait until 1928). Although women's neat work and dexterity had always been valued in the clothing and textile industries, few had reached the upper tiers of management. But there was a shortage of men in the years after World War I, as so many had been killed or maimed on the battlefields, and this, combined with the fact that teddy-bear manufacture was a relatively new industry and therefore lacked tradition, meant that women workers were offered opportunities they had rarely had before.

One of them was Norah Wellings, who, like Merrythought's Florence Atwood, began her career as a designer of soft toys at Chad Valley (indeed the women had worked together at that company). She remained in this position from 1919 to 1926, before leaving to set up her own factory, the Victoria Toy Works, also in Wellington, Shropshire. With the support of her brother, Leonard, whose business-management skills were essential to the project, Norah concentrated mainly on the design and production of cloth dolls, although she did include some teddy bears in her range. Her contemporaries often

remarked that Miss Wellings's creations were her whole life, and that she poured all her passion and enthusiasm into her work. Perhaps it was this great love for her subject that enabled her to produce dolls and bears that seemed to have more personality than many similar toys offered by larger firms in the same period.

Norah Wellings's bears are quite distinctive and a little unconventional, many of them sharing more

above and above left: *Norah Wellings Productions, 1930s. A cloth-bodied bear by Norah Wellings, shown with its label.*

characteristics with her dolls than with traditional teddies – they are often unjointed, dressed and with cloth bodies. Fortunately for today's collectors, she was strict in attaching to her products an embroidered label that read 'Made in England by Norah Wellings', and this was often accompanied by a swingtag (although these do not often survive). As her brother was heavily involved in the day-to-day running of the firm, it was understandable that when he died in 1959 she chose to wind up the business and retire the following year.

Much less experienced when she started out was E.M. Daniels, who worked for six months with various established toymakers before opening her own company, Jungle Toys, in 1914 in Earl's Court, London. From somewhat humble beginnings – at first Miss Daniels was assisted by only two fellow workers – the business grew to employ fifteen people by 1919 and exported worldwide. Her enchanting teddy bear designs played on the animal's cute looks, something that can be clearly seen in Bingo Bear, a koala launched in 1928 (koalas were at this time still thought to be members of the bear family). By maintaining her business at a manageable size and keeping her overheads down she was able to continue until the 1950s.

The efforts of two women also lay behind the foundation of a company called Pixie Toys. There is no record of their names, though it is known that they were the wives of two glass manufacturers whose business was experiencing difficulties. The women set up a modest soft-toy company in the 1930s, room

left: *Ealontoys, 1930s–40s, showing the distinctive square nose and heavy mouth.*

having been made available for them at the glassworks, and soon trade was flourishing. Elizabeth Simmonds, who had been an employee of both Norah Wellings and Merrythought, soon joined them as designer. Her contribution had a significant effect on the way Pixie bears developed: they share many characteristics with Merrythought and Farnell teddy bears, including webbed-paw claws.

Mrs Simmonds's involvement with and enthusiasm for Pixie Toys led her to buy the company from its founders, with a business partner, later in the 1930s. But during and after World War II demand for the toys fell away, forcing them to accept a takeover bid in 1955. The new ownership lasted only seven years, however, and the company closed in 1962.

Perhaps the firm with the most illustrious feminist pedigree was the East London Federation Toy Factory, founded in 1914 in Bow by the suffragette Sylvia Pankhurst, daughter of the more famous Emmeline. Its early products included a wide range of rag dolls, many of which were designed by artists commissioned from the Chelsea Polytechnic, and dolls with wax and china heads and limbs.

In 1921 Federation was dropped from the company name and in 1926 it registered Ealontoys as its tradename (later to become the company name in 1948). Production consisted predominantly of dolls until 1924, when teddy bears appeared in the catalogues. The bears, which were made using high-quality materials, were very successful, and by 1950 Ealontoys referred to itself as 'The Teddy Bear People' in all advertising material. The toys have a rather endearing quality, perhaps imparted by their heavy square noses and V-shaped mouths, which give them a rather solemn air – an Ealontoys teddy bear would never

laugh when you told him your troubles. Alas, along with many other small firms, the company experienced financial difficulties after World War II and was forced to cease production in the early 1950s.

Women were also writing about bears. Beginning in 1930, Gwynedd Rae wrote fourteen books about a little bear called Mary Plain, including *Mostly Mary* and *All Mary*. When compared to similar publications of the period, the books are refreshingly free from messages teaching children how to behave. Mary Plain is greedy

left: *Jungle Toys, Bingo Bear, c.1928. This koala may have been designed for the company's Australian customers.*

and rather conceited, enthusiastic and trouble prone, but the affection between the bear and the Owl Man, and between Gwynedd Rae and her characters, shines through each book.

GERMANY STRUGGLES TO CLAW BACK THE LEAD

When the Germans were defeated in 1918 they had to start rebuilding their economy from a position of

enormous disadvantage. In the Treaty of Versailles, 28 June 1919, it was agreed that territory would be ceded to France, Poland, Belgium and Czechoslovakia. On top of this, all German colonies were handed over to the Allied Powers to be administered under the newly formed League of Nations. This meant that Germany's former markets were suddenly much smaller. A further blow was the insistence that Germany should pay swingeing reparations (although these were later greatly reduced and payments stopped altogether in 1931 during the worldwide Depression). It was in this environment that the German teddy-bear industry had to regain the ground it had lost to British manufacturers during the war years.

After the war mohair remained very scarce in Germany and even when obtainable was hugely expensive. Consequently alternative materials had to be found if teddy-bear production was to resume. One solution adopted by Margarete Steiff GmbH was to use a cellulose plush made from nettle fibres. Known as the Brennessel Bär, the bear with this coat was rather uncomfortable to hold as the fibres were coarse and tweedlike. Some 19,556 examples were made between 1919 and 1921, and these are highly prized by collectors today for their novelty value. Another mohair-saving design involved dressing the bears in clothes so that mohair was needed only for the head and paws. Other bears were made with shorter and less luxurious mohair than prewar examples.

Although there was a short period after the war when Steiff returned to using boot-button eyes, as soon as glass

left: *Steiff, 1926. Dual mohair plush bears such as this were popular when they were launched and are highly sought after today.*

eyes were available again they became universal. Most bears of the early 1920s had clear glass eyes with brown painted backs and black pupils. Steiff's classic teddy remained very similar to the 1905 design – a bear with long arms, large feet with narrow ankles, protruding muzzle and humped back – but in 1921 it introduced kapok stuffing, and bears from that date on were plumper and lighter than before. In that same year Hugo Steiff introduced a conveyer-belt system, which speeded up production, although all of the work was still done by hand (as it is today).

In 1923, when German currency depreciation was at its worst, Richard Steiff decided to leave Giengen for the USA, with the intention of focusing on exports. His creative brilliance was irreplaceable, and later Steiff products certainly reflect the absence from the factory of this ingenious designer. The journey was made in reverse four years later when Ernst Steiff, the youngest of Margarete's nephews, returned from the USA to Giengen after fourteen years, to become executive secretary of the company.

Spirits needed to be lifted after the horror of the war, and once again Steiff read the international mood correctly, issuing during the 1920s a variety of lively, cheerful and spirited bears that could not fail to bring a smile to the lips of their owners. Some of these were dressed, including Teddybu, a white, golden or dark brown classic teddy bear wearing a colourful felt vest. Some had brightly coloured fur, such as Teddy Rose, a pink long-haired plush bear available from 1925. Others had the popular dual mohair plush, notably Happy, a golden teddy tipped with brown dye that was made in the mid-1920s. In 1989 Happy became for a while the most expensive teddy in the world when she was sold at

auction for a record £55,000. Among the more novel toys dating from this period was Tali Bär, introduced in 1925; a small bear waving a flag, he could be clamped to a bicycle as a mascot.

A completely original bear made during the Roaring Twenties, and epitomizing the mad energy of that age, was Harlequin, a 35cm (13 ¾ in) tall Steiff bear with one blue and one red side, one blue and one brown eye, and unusual yellow felt pads. It is thought that Harlequin was a sample that failed to pass muster, made by

above: *Steiff, 1928. Although novelty bears were in demand in the 1920s, Richard Steiff's classic teddy bear remained in fashion.*

above: *Steiff, Harlequin, c.1920.*
Limited edition replicas were made
for the Steiff Club in 2000.

right: *Steiff, Peace Bear, 1925,*
the prototype for the
company's Clown Series.

above: *Steiff, Teddy Clown, c.1926, a rare model due to its short production period.*

right: *Steiff, Petsy, c.1926, recognizable by his startling blue eyes and wire-framed ears.*

above: *Steiff, Teddy Babies, early 1930s, two of the first twelve sizes available of this popular design.*

1944 to mark her fortieth year with the company. As a one-off, Harlequin generated such excitement that he sold for £60,000 at the Steiff Festival in Giengen in 1999.

One of Steiff's most popular novelty bears was Teddy Clown, who was introduced in 1926. Available in eleven sizes, ranging from 23cm to 114cm (9in to 45in), and two different colours (tipped brown or golden), he was distinguished by his white pierrot's hat and ruff. Petsy, another wonderful design dating from this period, was remarkable for his startling blue eyes and pinkish-red embroidered nose and mouth. (A less desirable version with brown eyes and a black nose was also produced.) Petsy had large ears that, thanks to an internal wire frame, could be moved into various positions which would then hold. He was released in ten different sizes and as a glove puppet, as well as on a wheeled chassis as part of the Record Series.

Teddy Baby, designed in 1929 and released the following year, set the tone for the 1930s. This comical bear, with a cheerful friendly face, was first available in golden, dark brown or (until 1933) white mohair plush and in twelve sizes from 8cm to 45cm (3in to 18in). His glass eyes were set into the seam of the clipped mohair muzzle (the smaller sizes had muzzles made from velvet), giving rather a cartoonlike appearance, an effect that was amplified in the bears over 20cm (8in) in height, which had open mouths lined with flesh-coloured felt. Teddy Baby's arms were unusual in that when outstretched the paws faced downwards (in most bears the paws would face each other), while the large flat feet were reinforced with cardboard in order to improve the bear's standing ability. On its launch the range included eight sizes of Teddy Baby made of wool plush, but this line was withdrawn in 1933. The standard mohair plush bear

a worker in the factory. Certainly he was never commercially manufactured. Harlequin was rediscovered only recently, with documents supporting this theory of his origins. He was in the estate of a woman who worked for the bearmakers for more than forty years, five of them during the lifetime of Margarete Steiff. Proof of her employment included a wooden plate presented to her in

remained popular into the 1950s, however, encouraging Steiff to create several variations on the same theme.

Teddy Dicky appeared in Steiff catalogues between 1930 and 1936. He, too, had an inset clipped mohair muzzle, but his stitched mouth was extended by a huge smile that was airbrushed onto his face. He was available in twelve sizes from 10cm to 70cm (4in to 28in), in white or blonde mohair plush. Some Dickies had plain paws and soles of feet, but others were covered in velvet and painted with pads and claws. The Steiff archive holds two Dicky prototypes, never commercially made, that have snap joints in their paws, enabling them to hold small objects between finger and thumb. They are also capable of extraordinary head movements when operated correctly through their tails.

A similar bear to Teddy Baby was Circus Bear, which also had an inset muzzle, flat feet strengthened by cardboard to improve standing, and the distinctively angled paws. Patented in Heidenheim in 1935, Circus Bear had a clockwork mechanism that allowed him to move realistically (this mechanism had been developed by Steiff in 1910, but this was the first time it was used). From 1935 to 1939 some 897 Circus Bears were produced, their limited number making them highly prized by collectors today.

Accompanying many of these jolly characters were Steiff's pull-along and riding bears. The Roly Droly was advertised in its catalogues from the mid-1920s. When this wheeled toy was pulled, two bears (or other animals) on turntables would rotate in opposite directions. For a short time in the early 1930s a Teddy Baby on a wheeled chassis was issued as part of the Record Series. Most of the riding bears produced during this time had dark brown mohair coats, with a paler muzzle, and stood on all

fours, mounted on a red-wheeled chassis. A lighter coloured Young Bear was also available from 1939.

Steiff was an enlightened company, aware of its importance to the village of Giengen. Conditions at the factory were very good, with a state-of-the-art building, modern manufacturing methods and a subsidized canteen. There were also several apartments on site for married workers, which could be rented at reasonable rates, and an allotment scheme for employees to grow their own vegetables.

below: *Benchworkers in the Steiff factory in Giengen handmaking soft toys using methods still in use today.*

Unfortunately, many of these benefits had to be withdrawn during the late 1920s and early 1930s, when the worldwide economic Depression devastated the soft-toy market. Steiff had to decrease production and make several people redundant in order to stay in business. It also tried cutting overheads by using poorer quality materials on some of its bears. It began, for example, to

produce some lines in woollen rather than mohair plush. The most devastating result of the Depression in Germany was a profound political disillusionment which contributed to Adolf Hitler's National Socialist Party gaining power in 1933. This had an immediate effect on the German toy industry, with Ernst and Hugo Steiff, for example, being removed from their positions because of their Jewish sympathies.

A celebratory note was struck, nevertheless, in spite of the Depression, when in November 1930, Margarete Steiff GmbH celebrated fifty years of toymaking by issuing a small felt elephant, similar to the pincushion that Margarete had made for her friends all those years ago. This tradition was repeated at the seventieth and hundredth anniversaries.

During the 1930s minor changes were made to the design of Richard Steiff's classic teddy bear – the ears moved slightly closer together and he was given a slightly stockier appearance. To date a bear accurately, however, it is essential to look at the button and label whenever possible: the first buttons, produced in 1904, were embossed with an elephant. Between 1904 and 1905 a blank button was also used. From 1905 to the 1950s almost all buttons were embossed with the letters 'STEIFF', with the tail of the final 'F' underscoring some of the previous letters. The exception was some blank buttons made from 1948 to 1950 and painted blue (Steiff may have been reluctant to put its trademark on pieces that were of necessity of less than perfect quality). For a short period in the 1950s 'STEIFF' appeared in block letters without the underscore, while the vast majority of buttons produced after 1950 show 'Steiff' in cursive script.

Steiff teddies were also marked with labels, which were attached to the bear by the button. From around 1908 to 1925 a white label made from paper (or reinforced paper) was used. Between 1925 and around 1935 red-coated linen labels were used, then in 1933 or 1934 yellow labels were introduced. Labels have remained yellow since then, except for a short period in around 1950 when cream was used.

Despite the worsening political situation in Germany, Steiff remained ever quick to spot an opportunity. When Su-Lin, the first giant panda seen in the West, arrived at Chicago Zoo in 1937 the event caused a sensation, and Steiff launched a black and white jointed panda bear the next year. Perhaps it was Richard Steiff who made the connection between pandas and teddy bears. It is more than possible that he made the trip to Chicago, as he was living only a couple of hundred miles away in Jackson, Michigan. If so, it would have been one of his final bequests to the soft-toy industry, because he died in March 1939, aged sixty-three.

The contribution that Richard Steiff made to the teddy-bear industry cannot be overestimated, for he not only invented the teddy but also perfected its design. When he died, the clouds of war were gathering over Europe – perhaps it was a blessing that he was spared having to witness the company he had worked so hard for being brought low once again.

The outbreak of World War II in 1939 brought problems for the company that were as familiar as they were devastating. Materials such as mohair could no longer be imported from Britain and reserves ran very low. This shortage, coupled with the fact that all able-bodied members of staff were being called up for service, left production at the Steiff factory extremely limited.

opposite: Steiff, Teddy Dicky with plain (rather than painted) paw pads, 1930–6, shown alongside an early cinnamon bear.

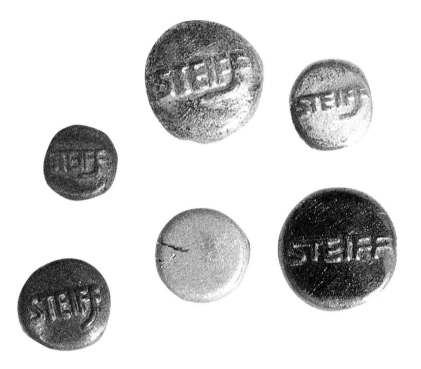

top left: *Nickel button used from 1905/6 to the mid-1920s.*
top middle: *Silver-coloured button (big) used from the early 1920s to 1950.*
top right: *Silver-coloured button (small) used from the early 1920s to 1950.*
bottom left: *Brass-coloured button used in the late 1930s.*
botton middle: *Blank button (bluish) used from 1948 to 1950.*
bottom right: *Silver-coloured button used from 1950 to 1952.*

In 1943 toy production ceased altogether as the factory was required to make military goods such as munitions and felt caps. The extensive Steiff archive was packed up and hidden away in various places, including the cellar of a local bowling alley. When the US Army occupied Giengen in 1945, some soldiers attempted to loot the factory; fortunately they left empty-handed.

At the Yalta Conference in February 1945 the victorious Allies divided Germany up into four Occupied Zones, with (very broadly) Russia in the east, the USA in south, France in the middle and Britain in the north. All four countries had a presence in Berlin. Steiff was in the US quarter, and from 1949 to 1953 all its bears bore a label marked 'Made in US-Zone Germany' attached to their right side. But first it had to resume production.

Drawing on experience from 1918, Steiff turned to the use of alternative materials, such as wool, cotton and synthetic plush, as well as producing clothed bears showing the minimum amount of fur. Although the Steiff team had sufficient fortitude to survive and continue with production as best they could, they could not control the lack of customers. The reduction in buyers was inevitable, as most people were preoccupied with rebuilding their lives, homes and country rather than with luxury toys. At the Leipzig Toy Fair of 1946 Steiff presented its first ten postwar products, all of which were made from artificial-silk plush. By 1948 the economy was recovering, and was soon growing at an incredible rate. When the first deliveries of mohair plush arrived in Giengen, Steiff once again began to make bears that would have met the exacting standards laid down by its founder.

Other German companies proved less resilient to the traumatic events of the first half of the twentieth century. Like Steiff, Gebrüder Bing chose to relaunch its range after World War I with a more cheerful bear. The 1920s Bing bear has a more pronounced clipped snout, bolder features, glass eyes and a smile. Sadly, while still producing high-quality teddy bears, Bing's struggle to survive the effects of war became an uphill task. It was one of the largest toy manufacturers in the world, but now its huge factory and large workforce meant that the overheads were too large and the structure too cumbersome for it to survive in the harsh conditions of world recession. The receivers were called in and production ceased in 1932.

Small companies were equally vulnerable in such turbulent times, often being far too reliant on a few customers or employees for their survival. One such, the Liegnitz Doll Factory (later known as Moritz Pappe), was founded by Arthur Pappe and Dr Curt Pappe in 1869. Little is known about the company's early years, as pre-1900 documentation does not appear to have survived, if it existed at all. Records from 1903 show a firm that concentrated on the manufacture of dolls, but seven years later it was making teddy bears, and by 1928 this had become its forte. Moritz Pappe's trademark, which was registered by 1907, took the form of a button embossed with a star.

Like so many teddy-bear manufacturers, Moritz Pappe was influenced by Steiff and produced a somersaulting bear similar to the latter's Purzel Bär, with an almost identical mechanism. Wisely, after World War I it registered its teddy bears for copyright, including, in 1921, special designs for movable bears. Unfortunately, no drawings or photographs of the bears have survived, so any information about them must be gleaned from the patent details. By this point Moritz Pappe bears had acquired a new clover-leaf button as their trademark.

The company catalogue of 1928 advertises a wide variety of bears, but it would appear that the star attraction of that year was the Baby Bär. When Steiff designed

right: *Steiff, Opera, 1920s. This beautiful white teddy bear was named by his owner, a German opera singer.*

right: *Gebrüder Bing, 1920s. With its clipped snout and upturned mouth this bear epitomizes the more cheerful designs produced by Bing after World War I.*

above: *Moritz Pappe, Baby Bär, c.1928. One of the earliest baby-style teddies to have been produced.*

left: *Educa, 1920s. The stitching on this bear's nose and mouth reveal the hand of Eduard Crämer.*

Teddy Baby in the following year it tried to copyright all baby bears. Its application was rejected, as Moritz Pappe had patented its bear in December 1928. Yet despite its success with Baby Bär, Moritz Pappe seems to have ceased production with the outbreak of World War II.

Eduard Crämer's Educa factory fortunately bounced back after World War I, reenergized by a range of new and exciting designs influenced by the Munich artist Marie Schultheis. Soon its toys were being sold around the world, particularly in the USA and England. This success ironically proved a drawback, for as a large proportion of the company's income came from abroad it was badly hit by the Depression of the early 1930s, when the collapse of the international economy caused huge reductions in exports. As Educa did not have a broad local sales base, it suffered. Quality was paramount to the company, however, and at no point did it compromise on workmanship, even though this might have encouraged sales at the lower end of the market.

The firm struggled on through the 1930s, but World War II put an end to all hopes of recovery. Like many soft-toy companies, Educa ceased production during the war, but, sadly, unlike others that quickly rallied, it experienced further difficulties during the

immediate aftermath. In 1945 Schalkau and the Educa factory fell into the Russian Occupied Zone, soon to become the German Democratic Republic (GDR), and, like many companies there, it was taken over by the state. The quality of the bears dropped considerably under the new regime, which was singularly ill-suited to producing toys named after a US president, and after eight years Educa closed down.

This story has a happy ending, though, for these wonderful bears were recently given the opportunity to rejoin the toy industry: with the full agreement of Eduard Crämer's descendants, Raby Rauensteiner Spielzeug GmbH have obtained the right to manufacture the Crämer bear once again. The Crämer bears produced today are in strict keeping with the original early examples, using primary patterns and high-quality mohair and materials, and carrying the Educa label.

One of Educa's chief competitors during the first half of the twentieth century was Schreyer & Co., often known as Schuco. The creative genius and energy behind this flourishing toymaker was provided by Heinrich Müller (1887–1958). He began designing playthings at a very young age, and by the time he was eighteen, aided by his brother, he was developing his ideas into actual toys. At the age of twenty-two he was employed by the world-famous toymaker Gebrüder Bing. His apprenticeship with Bing was short, however, because on 16 November 1912 he started his own company in Nuremberg, in partnership with furniture salesman Heinrich Schreyer.

Schreyer & Co. began by producing playthings for boys, such as tin soldiers and cars, but in 1913 it advertised its first soft toys, a range of wheeled animals called Tipp-Tapp-Tiere, which included a bear. Their originality and the quality of the workmanship ensured that they were quickly noticed by trade buyers and the public in what was becoming a highly competitive market. Müller dreamed of expansion, but his dreams were brought to an abrupt halt in 1914. When war broke out in Europe, the two partners were called up for military service and their premises were closed.

At the end of the war Müller was more determined than ever to become a successful toy manufacturer, but Schreyer seemed to have lost faith in the company and so left. By 1919 Müller had a new partner, Adolf Kahn, a textile merchant. Together they produced a range of imaginative novelty toys that sold through the difficult postwar years. The company's logo was a tumbling man clasping his legs, and in 1921 it registered the now internationally famous tradename Schuco. That same year it launched one of its most successful lines, the magical Yes/No Bear, at the Leipzig Toy Fair. This teddy's stumpy tail is actually a lever connected to a metal rod that is linked to the bear's head. When the tail is moved from left to right, the bear shakes his head; when it is moved up and down, he nods. The Yes/No Bear was immediately adored by the public, so much so that it remained in production until the company closed in 1976. During the intervening years a host of variations were introduced, including the Bell-Hop Yes/No, the Googly-Eyed Yes/No, Yes/Nos in various colours and the Clown Yes/No.

left: *Schreyer & Co., Bell-Hop Yes/No, 1926. The bear's tail is actually a lever that operates the head movement.*

The Yes/No Bear was just one of a range of novelty bears that Schuco introduced during the 1920s. Many had mechanical or clockwork mechanisms, revealing how much Müller had been influenced by Gebrüder Bing when he worked for that company. Perhaps the most profitable of the early Schuco lines, however, was the miniature range. Children love playthings that can be tucked in their pockets, and perhaps Schuco's experience in the toy-car industry made its designers realize how attractive a tiny bear would be to

below: *Schreyer & Co., 1927, a Schuco miniature pictured with its original box from a Bavarian handicraft exhibition.*

little hands. From around 1924 the company began issuing jointed bears that were only 6cm (2¼in) tall. Originally the miniatures were intended to be given away free as a marketing ploy, but they quickly became one of the firm's leading lines. The little bears had internal metal frames covered in coloured mohair plush, with felt paws and feet. Building on their success, Schuco adapted the idea to create a range of ladies' fashion accessories – miniature bears, available in lavish colours, that concealed items such as a perfume bottle, atomizer, lipstick, mirror or powder puff. By the end of the 1920s, thanks to this series of astute ventures, Schuco was able to move into a large four-storey building at Fürther Strasse 28–32, Nuremberg.

During the 1930s Schuco continued to adapt and expand its novelty range as well as making a number of larger more traditional bears (some with coloured fur), including a Baby Bear. In 1936 Adolf Kahn, who was a Jew, emigrated from an increasingly hostile Germany first to Britain and then to the USA. During World War II the Schuco factory, which had been turned over to the making of telephone equipment, was bombed several times. The company quickly recovered after the war, however, greatly aided by Kahn, who had established Schuco Toy Co. Inc. in the USA as the sole importer of Schuco goods. As a rule of thumb, Schuco toys that predate the war are marked 'Made in Germany DRGM', while postwar ones are lettered 'Made in US Zone, Germany'.

Schuco was just one of many soft-toy manufacturers, both little known and renowned, to

be based in Nuremberg. Prominent among the latter was Josef Pitrmann, whose exceptional Jopi bears and other soft toys were being produced from around 1911. The earliest toys were labelled with a tag marked 'Josef Pitrmann'. In 1922 the tag trademark changed to that of a bear with a Christmas tree. Later, in the 1930s, it changed again to a horse and rider beneath the words 'Very Fine Soft Toys, Jopi'.

Josef Pitrmann was most famous for his extremely popular musical bears, which he began to produce in the 1920s. The teddies had long brightly coloured mohair, distinctive orange and rather staring eyes, and concertina musical movements that could be activated by squeezing the stomach several times. At a time of intense competition between rival manufacturers, Josef Pitrmann's Jopi bears were much coveted when they were launched, and they remain so with collectors around the world today

Josef Pitrmann died in 1938, leaving his wife and daughter to continue the business. Little else is known

about the company, although it did present some brightly coloured musical bears at the 1959 Nuremberg Toy Exhibition that visitors remarked were the main attraction.

Making soft toys was traditionally a cottage industry in Germany, often involving the whole family. Skills were passed from generation to generation and from family to family through marriage. This was particularly true in toymaking centres such as Nuremberg or Sonneberg. Sometimes, as with Steiff, the firm remained intact and grew with the family. Alternatively it could father many smaller firms, as each child went in his or her own direction.

above: *Schreyer & Co., Bear Compact and Scent Bottle, 1920s, highly popular ladies' accessories produced by Schuco.*

The most famous example of the second model is the Hermann dynasty, members of which are still producing teddy bears today. In around 1907 in the village of Neufang, near Sonneberg, Johann Hermann (1854–1919) began making wooden toys, eventually founding Johann Hermann Spielwarenfabrik. He and his wife, Rosalie, had

Helmut, Artur, Werner and Horst. On his return, Bernhard was able to throw himself into bearmaking in earnest, producing a range of differently priced teddies – with something to suit all pockets – and successfully exporting them throughout the rest of Europe and the USA. One feature of these early bears was that they often had inset muzzles in clipped mohair, pre-empting Steiff's Teddy Baby. They also had rounder heads than many other German bears being made at that time.

BE-HA continued to grow until World War II, when three of Bernhard's sons joined up (the fourth, Horst, had died in 1937). After the war Sonneberg fell into the Russian Occupied Zone, destined to become the GDR, and from 1948 Bernhard Hermann began to relocate his company to Hirschaid – a town in the US Zone, midway between Sonneberg and Nuremberg and safe from state interference. Once there he changed the company's name to Gebrüder Hermann KG and began to tag his bears with the now-famous red seal that reads 'HERMANN Teddy ORIGINAL' and is still in use today.

A second famous teddy bear factory was founded by Johann Hermann's youngest son, Max. Before World War I Max helped his brother and sister, Artur and Adelheid, to run the family firm in Neufang. In 1920, after the death of his father, Max set up his own firm making teddy bears at the family home. Three years later he, too, moved to a factory in Sonneberg, with his wife, Hilde, and son, Rolf-Gerhard. The business now started trading under the name Max Hermann Sonneberg, with the trademark Maheso derived from the first two letters of each word. Bears were also labelled with green triangular swingtags, still used today, depicting a teddy bear walking a dog.

The typical Max Hermann bear of the 1920s and 1930s had an inset muzzle in a clipped mohair plush

six children, among them Bernhard, Artur, Max and Adelheid, all of whom were to become involved in the teddy-bear industry. It is thought that the first Hermann teddy bear was made in Neufang in 1913.

Bernhard Hermann, the eldest son, had married Ida Jäger in 1912. The couple moved to Sonneberg, where they started their own bearmaking business under the tradename BE-HA. During World War I Bernhard was called up for military service (with his brothers Artur and Max), leaving his wife to look after their four young sons,

different from the rest of the coat, large ears, a shield-shaped and horizontally stitched nose above a mouth shaped like an inverted Y, and long arms and legs with spoon-shaped paws and smallish feet.

Max Hermann, like his brother Bernhard, was forced to move premises after World War II. In 1949, when the GDR was declared an independent state, his son moved to Coburg, a town just across the border in the US Occupied Zone. There he set up a subsidiary company, Hermann & Co. KG. The suffering caused by the Soviet policy of collectivization of agriculture caused unrest in the East in 1953, and early that year Max fled to Coburg with his immediate family. The firm still operates from Coburg today.

Another fraternal affair was the company Gebrüder Süssenguth, founded in Neustadt, Bavaria in 1894 by the Süssenguth brothers, Wilhelm and Franz, to produce dolls' bodies and composite dolls' heads for the German toy industry. In the early 1920s the brothers tried to make a teddy bear using dollmaking techniques. The result, launched in around 1925, was a very unusual teddy known as Peter Bear. This fierce-looking creation had a mohair-covered head of pressed card with glass or wooden movable eyes in deep sockets, a black composite nose and a ferocious open mouth, filled with wooden teeth and a tongue. When the head was turned from side to side the eyes and tongue moved. Most had brown-tipped mohair plush fur, although they were also produced in apricot, grey and pink.

Given Peter Bear's rather unsettling appearance, it is not surprising that he met with little enthusiasm in the nursery. Consequently very few were produced. Almost half a century later, however, in 1974, approximately 100 examples were found in a disused warehouse in East Germany. They were all in mint condition, each in its original box, which, when added to their original rarity, has made them highly desirable to collectors worldwide.

Another Neustadt-based manufacturer was the Petz Co., started in 1921 by the Kiesewetters. This family were related to Conrad Reissmann, the founder of the Neustadt toy industry in the eighteenth century. Their early productions included teddy bears and soft toys made from quality mohair and felt. After World War I, in contrast to many other companies, the Petz Co. continued to use high-quality materials, despite the expense. Since 1947 the company's trademark has been a glass button stamped with the word 'Petz' in red.

The next generation of Kiesewetters was responsible for widening the range of toys being produced, adding a whole zoo, partly on wheels, to the already established classic teddy-bear range. Their most successful item in the post-World War II years was a teddy-bear school, launched in 1949, complete with classroom, teacher and eleven pupil bears. In that same year the firm attended its first Nuremberg Toy Fair, where it distributed its own toy magazine. In 1950, following the success of the teddy-bear school, a rabbit version was made available.

The Petz Co. was held in enormous respect by the industry, and its advice was called upon for a report on dangerous toys in 1953 (which discussed the use of eyes on pins – Petz used only eyes that were sewn or glued). Sadly, despite the esteem it had earned, the company fell into financial difficulties during the second half of the twentieth century and was forced to cut production, but it still makes some bears today.

opposite: Jopi, 1920s, an orange tipped musical bear that would play when its stomach was squeezed.

BEARS CROSS BORDERS INTO NEW TERRITORIES

During the early 1920s the USA was booming. New businesses sprang up every day in a market that encouraged innovation and enterprise. Immigrants from around the world came flooding to the Land of Opportunity (many of the younger ones clutching their teddy bears), helping to create a cultural mix undreamed of previously. All of this came to an abrupt halt, however, in October 1929 when millions of dollars were wiped off the stockmarket in the Wall Street Crash. Countless banks and business failed, and during the subsequent Great Depression unemployment rose to an unprecedented 13.7 million.

The US soft-toy manufacturers had to ride this economic rollercoaster, and many did not survive. Although they benefited from the embargo on imported German toys that was in place during World War I, the market almost dried up during the Depression when buying teddy bears and other luxuries was considered frivolous. Many makers went out of business, and those that remained had to run at a much reduced volume and aim their products at the cheaper end of the market. Lots of the complicated novelty lines disappeared during this period, as manufacturers and buyers alike favoured cheaper bears made from poor-quality materials. The situation improved radically in 1933, however, when new companies and new designs emerged across the country as a result of the social and economic reforms put in place by President Franklin D. Roosevelt and known collectively as the New Deal.

In 1923 Morris Michtom's son, Benjamin, joined the Ideal Novelty Co in New York. Over the next fifteen years he studied the trade closely, so that in 1938, when his father died, he was ready to take control of the company and, with his exceptional marketing abilities, transform it into one of the world's leading toy manufacturers.

Ideal bears changed very little during the 1920s and 1930s. They remained unlabelled and so today's experts have to look for typical Ideal features, such as the triangular-shaped head, to identify them. During the war years, when materials were at a premium, they were slightly thinner, reflecting the austerity being felt around the globe. In the 1940s the company produced a range of small unjointed bears, stuffed with kapok and given moulded resin noses, that foreshadowed the machine-washable 'safe' bears of the 1950s and beyond.

Competing with Ideal bears on US toyshop shelves were Knickerbockers. The Knickerbocker Toy Co. was founded in Albany, New York State, in 1850 to produce educational toys, such as wooden alphabet blocks and puzzles. Dutch settlers were known as 'knickerbockers' in New York, a tradition derived from Washington Irving's *A History of New York*, a fictitious account told by a Dutchman, 'Diedrich Knickerbocker', who wore rather outrageous puffed-out trousers. During the 1920s Knickerbocker turned to making soft toys. Its early bears had triangular-shaped heads with large, rounded ears and slightly flattened muzzles. Their bodies were often slimmer than those of European bears of the same period, and they did not have humps at the top of their backs. During the post-World War II years they acquired an inset muzzle, often made out of different material from the rest of the bear.

One firm that utilized every marketing ploy conceivable in order to outlast the Depression was the

opposite: Gebrüder Süssenguth, Peter Bear, c.1925. A fierce-looking bear that met with little success when launched.

above: *Commonwealth Toy & Novelty Co., Feed Me Bear, c.1937, with mouth open and ready to be fed.*

Commonwealth Toy & Novelty Co. Still operating today, it was established in 1934 by a Mr Greenfield. Like the Strauss Manufacturing Co. Inc., another New York-based firm, Commonwealth focused on the novelty-bear market. One of its most successful lines was the Feed Me Bear, launched in 1937. Perhaps not the most handsome of teddies, he appealed enormously to children because they could put things in his mouth. When a string at the back of his head was pulled his mouth would open; food could be fed through the metal mouth and emptied at a back opening. These bears, which continued to appear in the F.A.O. Schwarz catalogue until 1941, were often used to advertise consumables, and were displayed in grocery stores throughout the USA. The National Biscuit Co. used them to promote its animal crackers.

Across the Atlantic, while Germany and Britain were the two major European producers of teddy bears, other countries on the Continent began making the soft toys during the early decades of the twentieth century. The French were renowned throughout the industry for their mechanical bears and other animals, but they had no tradition of making soft toys. During the bear's boom years they imported teddy bears from Germany, beginning around 1908, but the outbreak of war in 1914, and subsequent border closures, brought an abrupt halt to German imports and kickstarted French teddy-bear manufacture.

Early French bears can often be recognized, even if they lack identification tags, by the poor quality of their workmanship. They were frequently made of inferior materials and were put together cheaply and hence badly. For example, they were often crudely jointed with a system of metal rods that was visible externally, their ears were frequently slotted into holes rather than embroidered on, and their eyes roughly sewn to the face rather than attached by wires. Such specimens have met with limited interest among collectors and within salerooms.

One of the first French companies to start producing teddy bears was the Paris-based M. Pintel Fils & Cie., founded around 1918. Pintel was also known for its mechanical dolls, caricatures and soft-toy animals, and to all its toys it attached a brass-plated button depicting a logo of two bears embracing one another – an image copied directly from a Steiff advertisement of 1906. The earliest Pintel bears are extremely elegant, with long slim bodies, arms and legs and a very slight hump at the top of their backs. After World War II the design changed dramatically, and they evolved into rather chubby teddies.

FADAP's bears also tended to be long and slender – indeed, the offspring of the two firms share many characteristics and are often mistaken for each other. The company, whose name stands for Fabrication Artistique d'Animaux en Peluche (Artistically Made Plush Animals), was founded in 1920 in Divonne-les-Bains, a small town close to the Swiss border, although it had additional offices in Paris. FADAP began production of teddy bears in the early 1920s, aided by the notable illustrator Benjamin Rabier, who lent his talents and ideas to the bear designs.

In the interwar years FADAP introduced bears in a variety of colours and materials, each one marked with an embossed metal button attached through a card tag to the left ear. During the war, when mohair was in short supply, it made a number of bears in flannelette. Although production continued after the war, the quality of the bears dropped dramatically, as did demand.

A third French teddy-bear manufacturer to emerge just after World War I was Emile Thiennot, who worked for Marcel Pintel before setting up his own soft-toy company in 1919 in direct competition with his former boss. He found a converted barn in the Champagne region of France to house his new company, and chose Le Jouet Champenois (Toys from the Champagne Region) as his trademark. Only one year later, in 1920, he was awarded a bronze medal by the Association of French Small Manufacturers and Inventors for his teddy-bear

right: *Petz Co., 1950s. Like all Petz bears made after 1947, this one is marked with a glass button bearing the company's name in red.*

designs. Emile's son, André, joined the company in 1949 and, at the time of writing – over fifty years later – he is still its president director general.

It was war that prompted another European country to start manufacturing teddy bears. Austria, united with Germany by the Anschluss of March 1938, was occupied by the Allies immediately after World War II, and it was in these conditions of defeat that the country's three most famous teddy-bear manufacturers – Berg, Fechter and Schwika – emerged.

Berg Spielwaren Tiere mit Herz GmbH, perhaps Austria's largest teddy-bear manufacturers and still in production today, was established in 1946 in Fieberbrunn in the Tyrol by the Broscheks. The family began making teddy bears using Army surplus materials – their coats were made from old Army blankets, with uniform buttons for their eyes and boxes of pebbles for their voiceboxes. As soon as more appropriate materials became available, such as mohair and glass eyes, the products improved and business expanded enormously.

Fechter Co. was also founded in 1946, in Graz, southeast Austria, by husband and wife William and Berta Fechter. Berta had worked as a teddy-bear seamstress in Neustadt during the 1930s, and was able to use her experience to make the toys out of whatever materials were available, including US Army surplus towels. By 1948 they were able to buy German mohair. Demand increased, and soon the husband-and-wife business had expanded to include more than twenty employees and a factory. Fechter bears are often confused with those of Schwika, a firm based in the same town whose bears are remarkably similar.

The Irish toy industry developed in a somewhat contrary fashion compared with that of its counterparts elsewhere. In 1938 Gaeltacht Services Division, a department within the Irish government, set up Gaeltarra Eireann, a government-funded department responsible for sponsoring, developing and supporting a toy industry that would create new jobs in the rural areas of the country's Irish-speaking region. Three factories were allocated to the department: one for dolls, one for lead toys and the third for the production of soft toys. The bear factory was based at Elly Bay in County Mayo and adopted the trademark Erris Toys, later to be changed to Tara Toys.

Ireland was one of the very few countries whose soft-toy industry prospered throughout World War II, for it held a neutral position and was therefore able to continue production when most other nations were forced to cease. During this time Ireland exported a large number of bears worldwide, meeting orders that its competitors were no longer in a position to honour. The bears resembled British bears of the period, although Irish bears were often of poor quality, being aimed at the lower end of the market. Those dating from 1938 to 1949 are marked with labels reading 'Made in Eire' (Eire being the name of the Irish free state), while those made after the declaration of the Republic in 1949 state 'Made in Republic of Ireland'.

On the other side of the globe, Australia relied on teddies imported from Britain throughout the early years of teddy-bear production and during the boom years. World War I prompted Australians to begin producing their own bears, although the high-quality mohair they used was still spun in Britain. The two most notable Australian firms, which inspired a great many smaller ones to form, were the Fideston Toy Co. and Joy Toys.

The Fideston Toy Co., which purported to be Australia's first teddy-bear manufacturer, was founded around 1917 by husband and wife Richard and Louisa Fiddes. This pair were running a book and music depot in Perth, Western Australia when Louisa noticed the absence of manufacturers of soft toys and teddy bears in the country and started making them herself. Her products were snapped up, and two years later the Fideston Toy Co. was registered, a factory was built in Perth and mass-production of soft toys began.

Another husband-and-wife team was responsible for the founding in the early 1920s of Joy Toys. Mr and Mrs Gerald Kirby, with the financial backing of their friend Daryl Lindsey, began producing teddies in South Yarra, Victoria. For the first ten years of its existence the company made top-quality jointed bears using British mohair. During the 1930s, however, it began to favour cheaper methods of production, including a fixed head structure (most traditional teddy bears have movable heads). This distinctive feature can be used to help identify Joy Toy bears when a label is lacking. Other characteristics are a somewhat unusual embroidered nose – often a little larger than necessary, with both final-end stitches longer than the rest – and arms tapering into pointed pads.

The years 1920 to 1949 saw the teddy become the most popular toy in the world. Unsurprisingly, the bear's development during this period is inextricably linked to the dramatic world events of the era, including recession, war and occupation. It is a mark of the teddy bear's resilience that these events, rather than crushing the young toy, caused new makers to spring up around the world. Some of these companies would be short-lived, but others would go on to challenge the supremacy of the traditional producers.

below: *Schwika, 1960s. This company's toys had an embossed metal button attached to the left ear by a piece of red cord.*

Literary Bears

Books and comics featuring bears were popular during this period, which saw the first appearance of two of the most famous teddies: Rupert Bear was created for the *Daily Express* by Mary Tourtel in 1920 and A.A. Milne's *Winnie the Pooh* was published in 1926. Gwynedd Rae's first book about Mary Plain appeared in 1930, and other teddy bears made appearances in novels, including Aloysius, Sebastian Flyte's ursine companion in Evelyn Waugh's novel, *Brideshead Revisited* (1945).

The most famous bear to emerge during the second half of the twentieth century was Michael Bond's Paddington, whose success may have sparked the creation of three new bear characters, all born in the late 1960s: Corduroy and the Gretz bears were both first seen in 1968 in the USA, while Bussi Bär was launched in Germany the following year.

1 *Michael Bond's original Paddington stories were illustrated by Peggy Fortnum, but, as the demand for images of the bear has increased, other artists have drawn him. Although each artist's Paddington is slightly different, the bear's hat, duffle-coat and Wellington boots ensure that he is unmistakable. In 1964 the first of fourteen specially written Paddington stories appeared in a BBC Blue Peter annual. The illustration reproduced here, which is by Harry Hargreaves, reveals its connection with this BBC children's programme ('bloo Peter bBc'). It also highlights one of the bear's greatest passions – marmalade sandwiches.*

2 *This montage of early teddy-bear memorabilia includes three books from Seymour Eaton's Roosevelt Bears series:* The Roosevelt Bears – Their Travels and Adventures *(1906),* More About the Roosevelt Bears *(1906) and* The Bear Detectives *(1908). The books were compiled from stories that first appeared in newspapers across the US, and were some of the first to benefit from the teddy-bear craze that was sweeping the country. Also shown are postcards and photographs of teddy bears, nursery books and a Winnie the Pooh boardgame dating from the 1930s that was produced by the English Teddy Toy Co. (in the US the game was made by Parker Bros.).*

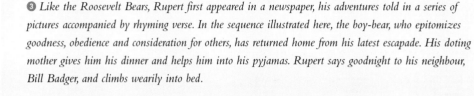

3 *Like the Roosevelt Bears, Rupert first appeared in a newspaper, his adventures told in a series of pictures accompanied by rhyming verse. In the sequence illustrated here, the boy-bear, who epitomizes goodness, obedience and consideration for others, has returned home from his latest escapade. His doting mother gives him his dinner and helps him into his pyjamas. Rupert says goodnight to his neighbour, Bill Badger, and climbs wearily into bed.*

4 *This illustration by E.H. Shepard shows Pooh and Piglet sitting on a gate singing a special 'Outdoor Song which Has To Be Sung In The Snow', which begins 'The more it SNOWS-tiddely-pom…'. It appeared in* The House at Pooh Corner *(1928), A.A. Milne's sequel to the hugely popular* Winnie the Pooh.

5 *Evelyn Waugh wrote* Brideshead Revisited *between December 1943 and June 1944 while on leave from military service recovering from a parachuting accident. When published the following year, it struck a chord with thousands of readers who, like Waugh, felt the loss of a golden age. In his preface to the revised edition of 1960, Waugh describes how the novel 'lost me such esteem as I once enjoyed among my contemporaries and led me into an unfamiliar world of fan-mail and press photographers'. Pictured below are Anthony Andrews and Jeremy Irons, stars of the 1981 Granada TV adaptation, with Aloysius – Sebastian Flyte's unpredictable teddy bear.*

chapter 4

THE BEAR BOOMERS

(1950–1964)

The 1950s and 1960s saw an unprecedented rise in the living standards of those in the West. This coincided with an equally remarkable rise in the number of babies born. The characteristics of the 'Changing American Market' were identified by Gilbert Burck and Sanford Parker in a series of twelve articles published between 1953 and 1954 in *Fortune* magazine and summarized as follows:

'It [the series] has analyzed the unforeseen and amazing rise in the American birth rate. It has recorded the unparalleled rise in the nation's living standards, and the postwar rise of a "great new moneyed middle class, growing larger, wealthier, more uniform and yet more various". It has described the economic implications of the phenomenal popularity of suburban life. It has examined individual markets, present and prospective, for cars, houses, food, appliances, clothes, luxuries and leisure-time spending.'

More babies and more disposable income had to be good for the toy industry, but competition within it was as keen as ever. This, after all, was the period that saw the introduction of Barbie (1959) and G.I. Joe (1964) or Action Man (1966). Teddy bears were already being seen by many as a traditional toy, loved by parents and therefore not quite as attractive to the novelty-hungry younger generation. The industry had to react fast in order to come up with a range of bears that would meet the needs of the age. Leading the way was Steiff in Germany.

The first signs of national recovery were apparent in Germany by the early 1950s, but the extent of the economic miracle, or *Wirtschaftswunder*, that was underway was beyond imagining. Between 1950 and 1964 West Germany's gross national product grew faster than that of any other European country; industrial output increased sixfold in the same period; foreign trade doubled between 1949 and 1950, and between 1954 and 1964 it trebled.

right: *Steiff, Zotty, 1950s. Even if it does not have its swing-tag, the Steiff Zotty can be recognized by its unique peach-coloured bib.*

Steiff knew that if it was to be part of this recovery it would have to update its range. It began by moving away from the traditional designs of Richard Steiff, treasured today, to a more modern classic teddy bear. Registered in 1950 and offered that year at the Nuremberg Toy Fair, the new-look teddy was definitely more bear cub than grizzly bear. Perhaps Steiff realized that children were growing up more quickly; fewer and fewer ten-year-olds would admit to loving their old friend (at least before lights out), so it had to aim for a younger audience. During the 1950s and 1960s the classic teddy bear's head became rounder and larger in proportion to the rest of his body, his muzzle became less pronounced and its fur was often cut short, his body became fatter and more youthful looking, and his limbs were less exaggerated in length and shape.

In the following year Steiff introduced Zotty, whose name derived from the German word *zottig*, meaning 'shaggy'. The original Zotty was covered with long curly brown-tipped mohair, with a peach-coloured bib inset into his chest. Like his predecessor, Teddy Baby, his felt paws pointed downwards and his mouth was open and lined with felt. There was also a much less popular Sleeping or Floppy Zotty, positioned lying down with closed eyes. The idea behind Zotty was to produce a much softer playmate for small children, an essential childhood friend that could be held and comforted, and that could comfort. Zotty was hugely successful and was imitated by many German firms, including Gebrüder

left: *Hermann & Co., Dancing Bear, 1960s. Despite its chain, this bendable dancing bear shows the influence of Steiff's Zotty.*

Hermann, Hermann & Co., Hans Clemens and Hugo Koch, all of which released shaggy bears with open mouths during this period. Those produced by Gebrüder Hermann were particularly similar and are often mistaken for Steiff bears today. The Hermann bears can be identified by their lack of a peach bib and a distinctive dropped stitch on each side of the nose.

Steiff teddies with clockwork mechanisms were also developed during this period, when the novelty bear was popular. Between 1950 and 1961 the company offered musical bears that played a tune when their key-operated mechanisms, which came from Switzerland, were activated. Then in 1951 Steiff reintroduced the Purzel Bär (Somersaulting Bear), which had first appeared in 1909 and had been produced until 1939. The new model, which was 15cm (6in) high and named Turbo Bär, met with limited enthusiasm and consequently only 814 pieces were made before it was withdrawn in 1953. A smaller version, only 12cm (4¾in) high, was also developed, but only made it as far as the archives. Steiff had a tradition of marking important dates in its history, and on 27 March 1953 it patented Jackie, developed to celebrate the fiftieth birthday of the teddy bear. This endearing bear cub was made using traditional materials but was much rounder and had shorter limbs and softer features than even the 1950s classic teddy bear. Jackie was available in four different sizes, and had two unique features that distinguish him from other bear cubs: a line of horizontal stitches in pink across his nose, and a belly button of dark brown paint sprayed on to the fur of his abdomen.

In 1958 the company celebrated another great event in the bear's history: the 100th anniversary of Theodore Roosevelt's birth. As a tribute to the US president who

had given the bear his name, Steiff made an exhibition piece, a life-size doll of Roosevelt on horseback which was paraded on a float at the first Bear Festival in Giengen, Steiff's home town, attractions at which included a parade, a touring exhibition of Roosevelt memorabilia and a children's party. A special brochure was printed depicting the Roosevelt doll surrounded by Nimrod bears, teddies dressed in hunting garb and carrying wooden rifles, first produced in 1953.

Although most German firms followed Steiff in producing softer and cuddlier teddy bears, a few chose to look backwards for inspiration. In 1954 Ernst Bäumler

above: *Steiff, Jackie, 1953, with original booklet, celebrating fifty years of the teddy bear.*

bought the company Johann Hermann Nachf., the original Hermann firm founded in Sonneberg in 1913 but now based in Munich. In buying the company, which he renamed Anker Plüschspielwarenfabrik, he also inherited all the models and designs, workers and machines. His partner in the business was Gisela Diehl, the wife of Ernst Diehl, a cartoonist, and sister-in-law of Ferdinand Diehl, who invented the popular animated hedgehog Mecki (turned into a toy by Steiff in 1951). The two partners parted company quite soon, though, and Ernst Diehl became actively involved with Anker, discussing new designs and gradually influencing the company to return to the classic Hermann range of bears. The classic designs were reintroduced together with characters such as Mufti the Laughing Donkey and Drolli the Grotesque Bear. By 1957 the trademark first used, an anchor with a bear, had changed to an anchor with a lion. Catalogues surviving from this period show a great variety of bears and other animals available.

SAFETY-CONSCIOUS BRITAIN

During the first half of the twentieth century the toy industry became increasingly concerned with safety and hygiene. Once the existence of germs was discovered, parents began to worry about what might be lurking in the fur of their child's cuddly companion. Philippa Waring describes in her book *In Praise of Teddy Bears* how these fears caused many parents to 'kidnap teddy bears, which were then

left: *Steiff, Nimrod, 1953. This special edition hunting bear was launched to celebrate the 50th anniversary of the sale of the first teddy bears.*

surreptitiously dumped as a health hazard ("Teddy's gone to fight that nasty Mr Hitler")'. One effect of this policy was that those few bears that survived the overaffectionate and sometimes wearing attentions of their owners and the attempts on their lives by their parents are often very valuable.

The person who did more than anyone else to improve the safety of teddy bears and other soft toys was Wendy Boston. Making soft toys had been Wendy's childhood hobby, and when her husband, Ken Williams, returned from the war in 1945 they started their own soft toy company in Crickhowell, South Wales. Three years later they patented the first screw-in safety eye, which was attached by a rust-proof nut behind the plush. These were intended to stop accidents in which small children choked on boot buttons or other types of sewn-on eyes.

Wendy Boston's most famous contribution to the toy world took another nine years to develop; in 1954 she test-marketed the first fully washable teddy bear (good-quality synthetic materials took a while to reach the market after the invention of nylon in 1935). The unjointed bear, with its improved safe eyes, was made out of nylon plush and filled with foam-rubber stuffing. The label recommended that it be 'washed in lukewarm suds'. When the teddies were launched on BBC television in 1955 they proved extremely popular. They were quickly imitated, but one typical and identifying feature of Wendy Boston bears is the design of the ears, which were often made out of the same piece of material as the head, allowing the bear to dry on the washing-line without fear of losing an ear. In 1960 the company changed its name to Wendy

Boston Playsafe Toys Ltd, and four years later it was producing 25 per cent of the country's teddy-bear exports. While production focused on these new bears, the company continued to make more traditional mohair jointed bears.

Like Steiff in Germany, Merrythought reacted to the demands of the new market by producing a range of novelty bears that would appeal to a new generation of children. To meet the increased demand for toys it extended the existing factory at Ironbridge and installed

left: Wendy Boston, Ted, 1963. One of the new generation of safe and hygienic bears that had screw-in eyes and were washable.

right: *Merrythought Ltd, Cheeky, c.1957, one of a new style of bears with a cartoonlike appearance.*

an automatic stuffing machine. (Hand-stuffing was not completely abandoned, however, and is still a method used today.)

In 1953 it produced a bear in red, white and blue to celebrate the coronation of Queen Elizabeth II on 2 June, just as Farnell had produced a similar bear when her father was crowned sixteen years earlier. Then, in 1957, it launched one of its most successful lines of the period – Cheeky. This bear, so named because of his wide mischievous smile, had a very round head with a large forehead. Sewn inside one of his ears, which were also very large and set low down on his head, was a metal bell, which rang when the bear was moved. Cheeky was first produced in mohair or artificial-silk plush, but in 1960 a nylon plush version was added to the range.

Merrythought was quick to recognize the future importance of tie-ins to the toy industry, and in the mid-1950s it made soft toys representing characters in the British comic *Robin*, including a bear. One of these little teddies, dressed in a red felt jacket and known as Mr Whoppit, became the mascot of the British car and speedboat enthusiast Donald Campbell. (The original character's name was spelt 'Woppit', but Campbell added an 'h'.) Together, in a series of vehicles called *Bluebird*, they broke the water-speed record seven times, reaching 444.7kph (276.3mph) in a turbo-jet hydroplane on Lake Dumbleyung, Australia, in 1964. In that year they also broke the land-speed record at Lake Eyre salt flats, Australia, with 648.7kph (403.1mph). They survived several spectacular crashes, but Campbell's luck ran out on 4 January 1967. On Coniston Water in England's Lake District a new world record was in sight, with an outward run of 466.7kph (290mph). But tragedy struck on the return when Bluebird's nose lifted, and with Campbell

and Mr Whoppit still inside, she plunged into the depths at 482.8kph (300mph). Campbell's last words, heard over the radio, were: 'She's tramping … the water's not good … I can't see much … I'm going … I'm on my back … I've gone.'

Until 2001 the *Bluebird*'s location in the depths of Coniston Water was unknown, but Mr Whoppit floated to the surface a few minutes after impact, buoyed up by

above: *Merrythought Ltd, Mr Whoppit, c.1956, seen with a photograph of Donald Campbell holding the teddy bear.*

Zealand. More recently Mr Whoppit has taken life more sedately with Gina, promoting water safety in New Zealand. The scars of his past adventures are there to be seen, however – his original blue fixed felt shoes were damaged in the fatal crash and had to be repaired. He also has an embroidered bluebird on his red jacket, a symbol added by Donald Campbell during their glory days.

Chad Valley, too, was keen to link its products with stars from television or radio. In 1952 it bought the rights to produce Sooty glove puppets, named after a little bear about to become very famous in Britain. (J.K. Farnell, Dean's and H.G. Stone were all producing teddy bear puppets at the time, but Merrythought did not produce its version of Sooty until 1960.) In 1948 an amateur magician, Harry Corbett, bought a teddy-bear glove puppet to amuse his children while on holiday in Blackpool, England. The puppet, which they named Teddy, soon became part of Harry's magic act. In 1952 success on BBC television's *Talent Night* led to regular appearances on the network's children's show *Saturday Special*. At this point Teddy received a makeover – his nose and ears were blackened and his name was changed to Sooty. In 1955 he was given his own programme, *The Sooty Show*, on which two years later he was joined by Sweep the Dog. Sooty acquired a girlfriend, Soo the Panda, in 1964, although the two were never allowed to touch on television. Harry Corbett died in 1975, but the following year Harry's son Matthew became Sooty's showbusiness partner. Sooty, Sweep and Soo were sold for £1.4 million in 1996 to the merchant bankers Guinness Mahon, whose intention it was to maximize their potential on screen and through merchandise.

In 1953 Chad Valley followed up its success with Sooty by producing Toffee, the Teddy with a Personality,

his kapok filling. The teddy bear's career did not end there. Campbell's daughter, Gina, continued the record-breaking tradition and Mr Whoppit became her mascot. He accompanied her when she broke the women's powerboat record, reaching 197.70kph (122.85mph) at Holme Pierrepont, England, in 1984, and again when she took the women's water-speed record in 1990, when she achieved 251.77kph (156.45mph) at Karapiro, New

whose adventures were featured in the BBC radio programme *Listen with Mother*. The Chad Valley bear was dressed in a bobblehat and scarf. J.K. Farnell also made a version of Toffee, although the first one did not appear until 1960 and was not dressed.

Chad Valley became a public limited company in 1950, a revenue-raising tactic that increased its ability to purchase existing companies and so expand further. Next on its shopping list was Hall & Lane Ltd of Birmingham, a manufacturer of metal toys, which it bought in 1951. In 1954 it swallowed Robert Bros., Gloucestershire, also a maker of metal toys, and yet another metal-toy company, Acme Stopper & Box Co. Ltd, Birmingham, became Chad Valley-owned in 1958. By 1960, when the company celebrated its centenary, it was employing more than 1,000 workers in seven factories.

H.G. Stone & Co. Ltd was responsible for another much-loved character of children's television, when one of its Chiltern bears was propelled from obscurity to stardom in the 1960s. How he came by his fame and some of his many adventures is described below by the late photographer Patrick Matthews:

'The name "Teddy Edward" goes back over thirty-four years during which time he has established his reputation as one of the most travelled teddy bears in the world. He has been to Timbuktu in the Sahara Desert, to Katmandu en route to Everest, and to the bottom of the Grand Canyon as well as New York City and many European countries including the Greek Islands.

But how did it start?

I was working with Cecil Beaton on a photographic project in his Wiltshire garden and I took a photograph of his cat Timothy White sitting in a bed of nettles. Enlarged and framed we hung it in our three-year-old daughter's bedroom. This gave Mollie [Patrick's wife] the idea of photographing some of Sarah's [his daughter's] toy animals to join Timothy White on the wall. From this, the next step was to write simple stories about Teddy Edward, Snowy Toes the panda, Bushy the bush baby and Jasmine her rabbit.

Once the adventures started, with Sarah herself in the earliest books, other bears and animals drifted in and out of the books and films.

We produced nineteen titles, plus reprints, twelve films for the BBC's *Watch with Mother* series narrated by

below: *Photograph of Teddy Edward on location in the Sahara Desert for the* **Watch with Mother** *television series.*

Richard Baker, postcards, jigsaws, etc. and two years of *See-Saw* magazine, which carried a photographic story about Teddy Edward each week.

The early books, predominantly black and white, were centred around children's holidays at the seaside (Cornwall and Norfolk), on a farm in Dorset, and later further afield in France, Spain and Greece.

In the Sahara, Teddy Edward and I travelled 500 miles [800km] down the River Niger in a *pirouge* [a hollowed out tree trunk made into a boat] and slept out under unbelievably bright stars each night. I went to India with my daughter, Sarah, now grown up, on our way to Everest where at 13,000 feet [4,000m] we were staying in a Japanese hotel which gave us a vivid memory of the fiery tip of Everest, the last light we saw that night, the top of the world. That was the highest place in the world, the Grand Canyon one of the deepest. Mollie and I booked to ride to the bottom of the canyon on mules to spend the night at Phantom Ranch. The American girl who took our booking said she had been in London a few weeks earlier and had bought all the Teddy Edward books and was enchanted to meet him in person. Enchanted may not have been the word Teddy Edward used to travel to the bottom of the canyon, as he had to sit in the guide's saddlebag, but he was given a certificate for getting to the bottom and back.

Teddy Edward was always photographed in natural poses and in situations children would understand, and we purposely never dressed him up … except in the mountains where [he] proudly wore his Nepalese coat against the cold which was given to him by his panda friend Domtuk (Snowy Toes' twin) who wore one like it.

Peter Bull [an actor, arctophile and author of *Bear with Me*] became a friend and mentioned Teddy Edward

in his books, and Colonel "Bob" Henderson [president of the Teddy Bear Club] was a huge admirer too. He wanted me to take over Good Bears of the World [a charity providing teddies for children in hospital] when he was beginning to find it too large a commitment. Sadly, I was too busy to be able to do this.'

In December 1996 Teddy Edward was sold at Christie's in London to Yoshihiro Sekiguchi, president of the Japanese toy company Sun Arrow, for £34,500 and is now on display in one of his teddy-bear museums.

On Christmas Eve 1956 a young BBC cameraman called Michael Bond was shopping in a London department store for a present for his wife. As he recalls in *Something About the Author*: 'On one of the shelves I came across a small bear looking, I thought, very sorry for himself as he was the only one who hadn't been sold. I bought him and, because we were living near Paddington Station at the time, we christened him Paddington.' A few days later Michael Bond was sitting at his typewriter, seeking inspiration for a story he was trying to write, when he noticed the bear and was inspired to type the opening lines of *A Bear Called Paddington*: 'Mr and Mrs Brown first met Paddington on a railway platform. In fact, that was how he came to have such an unusual name for a bear, for Paddington was the name of the station.'

Once published, the book about a scruffy little bear in Wellington boots and a duffle-coat was an instant success. The story of how he was found by the Browns sitting on a suitcase near Lost Property wearing a label around his neck that read 'PLEASE LOOK AFTER THIS BEAR. THANK YOU' has been translated into nearly

opposite: *Harry Hargreaves' drawing shows Paddington surrounded by his favourite things on Christmas morning.*

right: *Dean's Rag Book Co. Ltd, Tru-to-Life, c.1955, a realistic-looking bear whose design was the result of painstaking research.*

thirty foreign languages and has been followed by another ten novels, two collections of short stories, dozens of picture books, television animation and soft toys. Today he is probably – after Pooh – the second most famous bear in the world.

The interest in pandas and polar bears seen in the 1930s and 1940s showed that there was a demand for lifelike bears, and in 1955 Dean's Rag Book Co. tried to build on this by producing a realistic-looking grizzly bear cub. Known as Tru-to-Life, the bear was the idea of Sylvia Wilgoss, who joined Dean's design team in 1952 and worked closely with chief designer Richard Ellet, succeeding him in 1956. Tru-to-Life was created after extensive studies of the real North American grizzly bear, and was an unjointed bear capable of sitting, standing or even walking on all fours with the help of a collar and lead. Although he was a very natural-looking bear, he was made from up-to-date materials, with acrylic plush fur, pink rubber paws and feet, and a moulded rubber nose on a white acrylic plush muzzle. A white version of Tru-to-Life that looked remarkably like a young polar bear was also produced. The attention to detail in their construction, and their relative rarity, mean that both bears are highly sought after by collectors today.

NEW-LOOK BEARS IN THE USA

The USA was the powerhouse behind the West's desire for change in the 1950s, and the US market was at its most experimental at this time. Those companies that were to survive and grow in the next two decades embraced the latest materials and designs, recognizing the importance that film and television were having on the nation's culture – many of the most successful US teddy bears from this period have a cartoonlike appearance.

One company that went from strength to strength, and is still flourishing today, was the Gund Manufacturing Co. Founded in 1898 by German immigrant Adolph Gund, this company was based in Connecticut before moving to New York, where it produced novelty toys. It is believed that teddy bears joined its range in 1906, but these early examples are true rarities. The credit for Gund's success can be given to Jacob Swedlin, a Russian immigrant, who joined Gund in 1909 as a porter when he was only fourteen years old. Swedlin became interested

left: *Knickerbocker Toy Co. Inc. 1950s. This bear's large head and eyes give it a babyish look. The dungarees are not original.*

in soft-toy production and his enthusiasm and hard work were soon noticed and rewarded. He was trained in cutting, patternmaking and design before becoming Adolph Gund's personal assistant. Gund had no children of his own, so when he retired in 1925 he sold the company to Swedlin for a token sum. Soon after this purchase three of Swedlin's brothers joined him to help manage and develop J. Swedlin Inc. (the company name changed in 1925, although they kept 'Gund' as their tradename).

After World War II it enjoyed enormous success, aided in 1948 by Walt Disney granting it exclusive rights to produce soft-toy versions of Disney animations. It went on to produce stuffed versions of King Features and Hanna Barbera cartoon characters, including the latter's Yogi Bear. This cheerful park inhabitant, named after the US baseball player Yogi Berra, was a huge success when he was introduced to US television viewers in the 1960s, guaranteeing sales for Gund's merchandise. Gund was also among the first US firms to produce teddy bears with inset vinyl faces, along with Ideal, Knickerbocker and other less well-known companies.

Following an almost identical path to Gund was the Ideal Toy Corporation (formerly Co.) in Brooklyn, New York. It, too, formed important relationships with well-known character bears, including in 1953 a Smokey the Bear soft toy. Smokey was introduced in 1944 as the symbol of the US Forest Fire Prevention Campaign. He was drawn by Albert Staehle, a noted illustrator of animals, and named after Smokey Joe Martin, a famed New York City firefighter. In 1953 Ideal won the licence to manufacture Smokey Bear models, and produced a range

opposite: Japanese, Small Bear School, 1960. This set would have undercut similar European products.

of hugely popular dressed bears with vinyl faces and paws. Some of the toys even issued a fire-safety message when prompted. In 1968 Ideal lost the Smokey licence to Knickerbocker, which went on to make the bears until the late 1970s.

NEW BREEDS OF NOVELTY BEARS

The 1950s and 1960s were the era of the novelty bear, and this meant that Japanese manufacturers – which had been producing moulded, bisque and celluloid teddies since the 1920s – came into their own. (Pre-World War II soft plush/mohair teddy bears from Japan are, however, a rarity and often lack labels even when identifiable.) After its occupation by the US Army (1945–50) Japan became active in the toy industry and soon led the way in respect of technological and mechanical toys. In the 1950s firms such as the Kamar Toy Co. produced clockwork and battery-powered teddy bears that were both innovative and cheap – a combination that caused many established European and US manufacturers much anguish.

Switzerland was also known for its clockwork movements. Indeed, before World War II the Swiss had provided musical boxes to be fitted inside the teddy bears of all the leading manufacturers. In the early 1950s, however, the first Swiss teddy-bear manufacturer was established in Zurich. MCZ adopted the trademark Mutzli, which means 'little bear', and used the name on identification tags attached to the toy's ear or chest. The range included dressed boy and girl bears, bear rattles and soft-filled unjointed bears for newborns, a Chef Bear, bears with flexible limbs and bears on all fours. Later examples of Mutzli bears can be found with labels depicting a new tradename, Felpa. Sadly, the firm went out of production in the 1990s.

SMALL BEAR SCHOOL

A complete darling school of 6 pupil
b... teacher bear. Has large
... slates, etc. A brand
... rs.

Made in Japan

Novelty Bears

Novelty bears were popular throughout the 1950s and 1960s, musical bears, dressed bears, bears on bicycles or rollerskates and talking bears all winning admirers. Merrythought's Cheeky design, so named because of the teddy's wide smile, was much copied, as was Schuco's relaunched Yes/No bear, first seen in 1921 and now rereleased as Tricky. Many of the most innovative clockwork or battery-operated designs came from Japan.

❶ *In 1965 Merrythought introduced the Twisty Bear Family: Mr and Mrs Twisty Bear and their two children. Over their blue fabric bodies father and son wore red dungarees, while mother and daughter wore red skirts and white aprons. All the bears had large feet, which allowed them to stand, and an internal wire frame. The latter meant that if twisted the bears would hold a position until moved again. In 1966 Merrythought launched the Twisty Cheeky Family, a mixture of the Twisty Bear and Cheeky lines.*

❷ *In the first three years following World War II most forms of Japanese industry were discouraged by the Allies. Following a policy change in 1948, and the withdrawal of the occupying US army two years later, Japan thew itself into manufacture. During the 1950s and 1960s tinplate, clockwork or battery-powered toys began to flood the US and European markets. Although Japanese quality often fell short of that of the established manufacturers, Japanese prices were dramatically lower. This clockwork bear, which dates from the 1960s, ambles forward when wound up. Like many Japanese products of the time, it comes in a cardboard box whose lid is beautifully painted with an idealized view of the contents.*

3 Musical bears with clockwork or pressure-activated mechanisms were popular from the 1920s. Teddy manufacturers around the world tended to buy their mechanisms from Swiss producers rather than attempting to make them themselves. Steiff introduced musical teddies in 1928 with Musik Teddy and Musik Petsy. This example dates from around 1950, when dressed bears were highly popular. Its skirts hide a cylinder containing the musical movement. When the bear was pressed down, the melody would play.

4 In the first two decades of the twentieth century, during the height of the teddy bear craze, images of the toys decorated an enormous range of everyday household objects and luxury goods. Fun clothing and accessories made out of mohair plush and with a teddy motif, such as this child's purse, were also popular. Dating from around 1910, it is shown with a photograph of its original owner – a little girl who is obviously determined to keep her treasured purse close by her side as she poses on the family sofa.

5 One of the finest producers of novelty teddies was Schreyer & Co., which, under the brand name Schuco, introduced a wide range of automotive, miniature or otherwise unusual bears to the market, using many of the ingenious techniques it had developed as a producer of toy cars. This uniformed soldier bear from the 1920s, the clockwork Bär 155 Automatic, would march up and down when wound up. Like all automotive toys, its value is greatly increased by its working mechanism, although this model is genuinely rare and so always sought after by collectors.

chapter 5

THE BEAR SLEEPS

(1965–1979)

The period from 1965 to 1979 was a disastrous one for teddy-bear manufacturers – dozens of traditional toymakers went out of business during what was probably the biggest shake-up the industry had ever seen. Despite the resilience of a handful of the finest manufacturers, the future of the teddy bear began to look very precarious, for a number of reasons. Firstly, the birth rate was falling. Companies had expanded during the baby boom to meet the demands of a growing population, but now they had either to retract – not very easy when many had invested in new buildings, equipment and people – or to develop new markets. Secondly, the customer base had changed. Traditionally toys had been bought by parents or grandparents, but by 1965 children were becoming consumers in their own right – and they were not buying teddy bears. Instead they were spending their money on, or making demands for, the hundreds of new and exciting-looking toys being advertised on commercial television.

opposite: Unjointed bear, late 1960s, with plastic eyes and nose, wool/ synthetic mixed plush. Maker unknown.

Thirdly, by 1965 there were few companies that focused exclusively on teddy bears or even soft toys. Most also produced puzzles, board games, toy cars and dolls. All these products were vulnerable to the vagaries of a changing market during the 1960s and 1970s, and if one range did badly, it would often bring down another, more successful range, with it. For example, as well as owning Pedigree Soft Toys Ltd, which had factories in Northern Ireland and New Zealand, and, from 1966, the Australian teddy-bear manufacturer Joy Toys, the British company Lines Bros. Ltd was also responsible for household names such as Hornby, Dinky, Meccano, Tri-ang and Scalextric. When Lines Bros. ceased production in 1971, its prices consistently undercut by toy-car manufacturers from

Southeast Asia, it took Joy Toys with it. Pedigree bears were fortunate to survive the closure, as soft-toy production was transferred to Canterbury, England, and taken over by Dunbee-Combex-Marx the next year. But this was only a temporary stay of execution – Pedigree finally closed its doors in 1988.

A fourth reason why the teddy-bear industry was under great pressure during this period was the emergence of multinational toy companies. Up to the mid-1960s home brands had been dominant in those countries, such as Germany, Britain and the United States. with a tradition of toymaking In the UK, for example, toyshop shelves were filled by Lines Bros., Chad Valley, Britains, Mettoy (with the Corgi brandname) and Lesney (Matchbox), with only a few cheap imports from Hong Kong. The enormous success of Hasbro's soldier-doll G. I. Joe, which was licensed to the British company Palitoy as Action Man in 1966, heralded the arrival of the multinational. Soon all new toys were being heavily marketed and were expected to please an international audience. As toy manufacturers searched desperately for the next G.I. Joe, they tended to overlook traditional toys such as the teddy bear.

Finally, as toy manufacturers became increasingly driven by fashion, highly skilled workforces producing premium-quality toys intended to last became less attractive than cheap labour making 'toys of the moment' to be marketed and sold internationally. Since the 1950s Western companies had been under pressure from cheap imports from Hong Kong and Japan. Now many US and European manufacturers moved production to Southeast Asia in order to match foreign competitors' prices.

The list of companies that were casualties of these developments makes depressing reading. In the mid- to late 1960s, the Nuremberg manufacturer Schuco experienced a heavy fall in sales of tinplate toys, largely due to competition from the up-and-coming Japanese toy industry. This unavoidably had an effect on its entire business, including soft toys. Despite the success of its Bigo Bello Series of teddy bears in the 1960s, Schuco was forced to declare bankruptcy in 1976. Schuco had begun to collaborate with Ernst Bäumler's Munich-based firm Anker in that year, and when it fell it took the smaller company with it.

Britain lost two of its oldest and most revered toy companies during this period. In 1964 J.K. Farnell had moved production to Hastings, Sussex, and leased its London Alpha Works to a new company, Acton Toycraft Ltd, whose trademark was A Twyford Product. Despite such cost-saving measures, Farnell closed for business four years later, while Acton Toycraft ceased production in the mid-1970s.

Perhaps one of the most surprising casualties was The Chad Valley Co. Ltd, which had been very active during the previous decades. In 1967 Chad Valley acquired H.G. Stone & Co. Ltd, producers of Chiltern Toys, to become the country's biggest soft-toy manufacturer. With this purchase a proportion of soft-toy production moved from Wellington to Chiltern's factory based in Pontypool. After the takeover many Chad Valley teddy bears adopted a new label that read 'Chad Valley Chiltern Hygienic Toys Made in England', despite being manufactured in Wales.

Unfortunately Chad Valley stretched itself too far, and when depression hit the industry in the 1970s the company was vulnerable. Throughout the early 1970s it made valiant attempts to restructure, but these endeavours failed, forcing acceptance of a takeover bid by Palitoy in 1978. The name Chad Valley was acquired in 1988 by Woolworth's, which still uses it to market a range of toys produced in the Far East, including low-quality teddy bears which do not closely resemble the Chad Valley bears of old.

A third British company that failed to survive was one that had done more than any other to update the

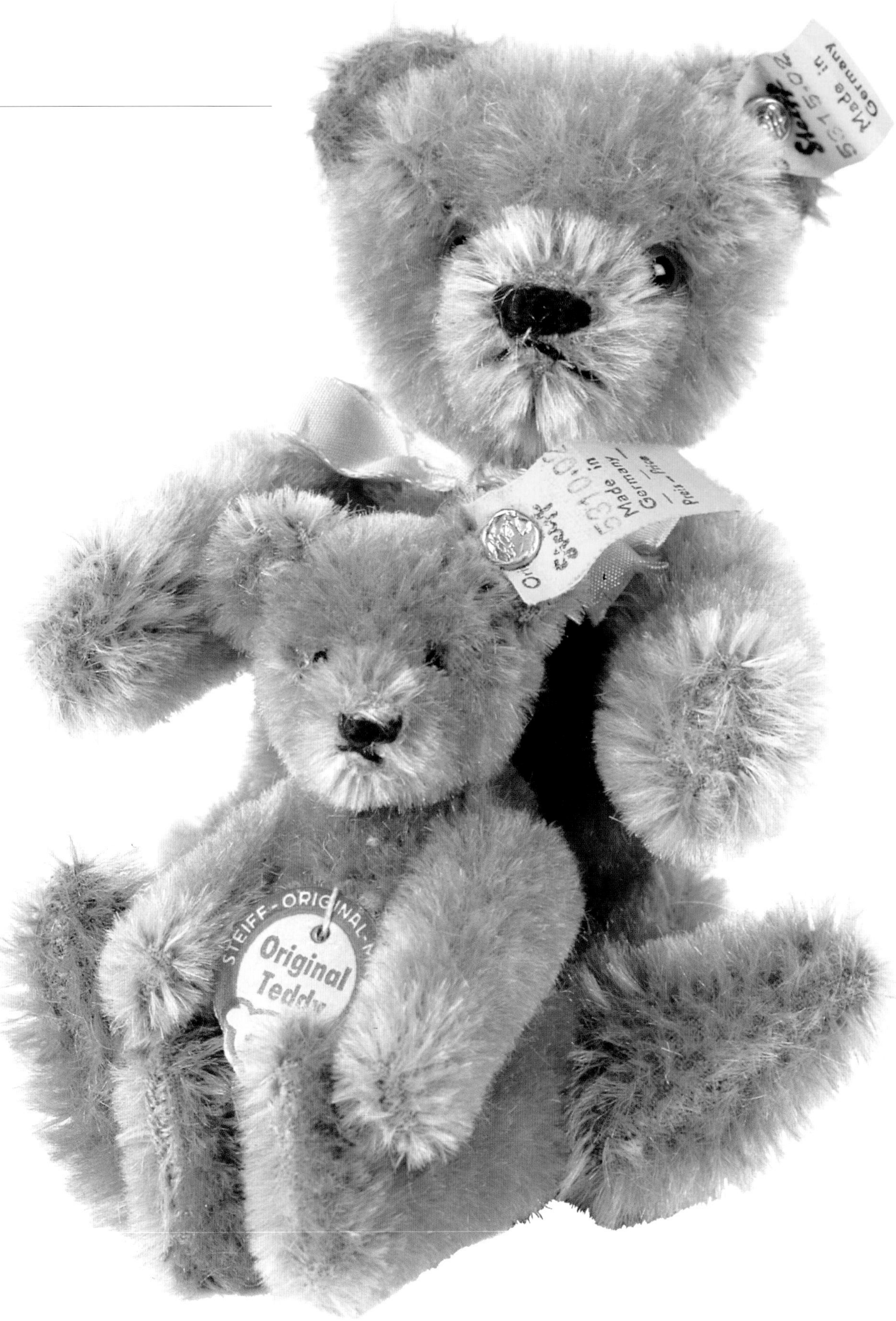
Made in Germany
Original Teddy

teddy bear during the second half of the twentieth century. Wendy Boston Playsafe Toys Ltd was bought by Denys Fisher Toys in 1968, and the factory closed nine years later.

The USA, too, had its share of casualties, including one of the oldest teddy-bear manufacturers in the world. By 1968 the Ideal Toy Corporation, now a publicly owned company, had factories in New York and New Jersey and was producing and distributing in countries around the world, including Japan, Australia, New Zealand, Canada, Britain and the rest of Europe, employing more than 4,000 people. During this great expansion the company did not forget its place in the history of the teddy, keeping as its motto 'Excellence in Toy Making Since the Teddy Bear'. But even this market leader could not withstand the pressures of the time and, in 1982, it was sold to CBS Toys.

The Ideal Toy Corporation had played a vital part in the teddy bear's triumphant conquest of the USA in the early part of the twentieth century. It is difficult to understand why, therefore, when Mark Michtom (grandson of the co-founder of Ideal, Morris Michtom) handed over the reins to CBS, the latter chose not to include teddy bears in its range.

As the traditional teddy-bear manufacturers floundered, new companies mushroomed, particularly in the USA, to produce cheap soft toys and other products meant to be given as presents. Rather than being treasured friends, these bears were, for the most part, token gifts that would often accompany a bunch of flowers or a box of chocolates. Some clutched red hearts and declared 'I Love You!', while others advertised products such as fabric conditioners. The most successful of these new companies was Russ Berrie & Co. Inc., which was founded in 1963

and had its headquarters in New Jersey, production plants in Korea and China, and sales around the world. Russ built its success on being able to react quickly to the changing gift industry, while keeping overheads down.

Those companies that did survive this traumatic period in the toy's history tended to be traditional teddy-bear manufacturers with a premium product that people were prepared to pay more for. Most important of all, they were not made vulnerable by the failure of other lines (people continued to buy teddy bears throughout the twentieth century, although the popularity of the toy fluctuated enormously). The five companies that best matched these conditions, and are now considered to constitute a sort of worldwide teddy-bear aristocracy, were Steiff, Gebrüder Hermann, Hermann-Spielwaren, Merrythought and Dean's.

In Germany Steiff continued to produce hand-finished soft toys in its Giengen factory, rather than being

opposite: Steiff, Original Teddies, c.1966. Not all of the new-look bears had heart-shaped muzzles.

tempted to cut costs and move production overseas. In 1966 it updated Richard Steiff's classic teddy bear once more, this time taking a radically new direction – the mohair around the eyes and muzzle was clipped short, forming a heart shape. The bear also lost his hump, and his legs were much shorter and fatter than his predecessors'. On 10 February 1966 he was registered under the name Original Teddy. During the 1960s and 1970s Steiff produced a range of bears in both Draylon and mohair plush – Cosy, Lully, Molly, Petsy, Zooby and Tapsy; some were jointed, while others were soft floppy teddies intended to be cuddled by a young child.

Further northeast in Bavaria, Gebrüder Hermann KG remained in family hands during the 1960s and 1970s and continued to make both traditional and more up-to-date

Peter Bull's miniature teddy bear Theodore, sitting in his chair, reading.

the company in 1972 after studying engineering. That same year saw the arrival of Jacqueline Revitt, who was later to become chief designer and whose attention to detail would have made Florence Atwood proud. With brilliant design skills, enhanced by a romantic imagination and a keen understanding of real animals and their environments, Jacqueline Revitt and Oliver Holmes have continued to add magic to Merrythought.

In the early 1960s a subsidiary of Dean's Rag Book was formed, Dean's Childsplay Toys Ltd, and in 1965 this was adopted as the name for the whole company. Dean's strengthened its position in the teddy-bear market in 1972 when it took over Gwentoys Ltd, a traditional bearmaker based in Pontypool and founded in 1965 by three former managers of the nearby Chiltern factory. The Dean's/Gwentoy Group tended to concentrate on the lower end of the market, while Dean's Childsplay continued to produce first-class bears, a combination of activities that helped to ensure their success.

The pop culture of the 1960s and early 1970s ironically imbued in many people a sentimental longing for lost times – perhaps as a reaction. This sense of nostalgia was a key factor in the emergence of the heritage movement, which is still in force today. Companies such as Crabtree & Evelyn and Laura Ashley drew on the past – or rather on an idealized interpretation of the past – to produce goods that had an old-fashioned and reassuring quality. The marketing of teddy bears as adult collectables, which began very slowly in the 1960s then grew to dominate the traditional market, can be seen as part of this movement.

In 1964 the toymaker Margaret Hutchings published *Teddy Bears and How to Make Them,* which included a brief history of the toy. This was followed in 1969 by *Bear with*

designs. Management of the business transferred to the next generation in 1986 when the four daughters of Artur, Werner and Helmut took over the day-to-day running of the firm. Likewise, the granddaughter of Max Hermann, Dr Ursula Hermann, became a director of Hermann-Spielwaren GmbH in 1983, followed a decade later by her brother, Martin.

In England Merrythought continued to enjoy success as a highly respected toymaker under managing director Oliver Holmes, the son of B. Trayton Holmes, who joined

Me, written by the actor and collector Peter Bull after his request on NBC's *Today* programme for some interesting teddy-bear stories – he received more than 2,000. The success of these publications proved that there was a huge number of secret arctophiles in the world, all wanting to collect bears or bear memorabilia. Bull himself already had a large hug of bears ('hug' being the collective noun for teddies), including Delicatessen, later to star as Aloysius in Granada TV's landmark production of *Brideshead Revisited*. His favourite teddy, and life-long companion, was Theodore, a miniature bear only 10cm (4in) tall that went with him everywhere in his top pocket. Peter described the central role that Theodore played in his life in the following passage:

'Only one Teddy can take first place in one's affections, and despite the material success of such personalities as Aloysius and Bully Bear [the bear Peter developed with House of Nesbit], Theodore is The One. He has been with me longer than any of the others, and was given to me to celebrate a first night by my friend Maurice Kaufman. I fear I took him for granted from the word "go". I have carried him in my pocket everywhere.

To me he is factual and as real a part of my life as anything I possess. He doesn't remotely resemble a favourite watch or any really inanimate object, but I would no more dream of going away without him, even for a night, than flying to the moon. But then I never really fancied that, though I think Theodore might rather like it. Yet I know that the same thing would happen on

right: *The young 'Bob' Henderson, pictured in fancy dress, with his 1904 Steiff bear, Teddy Girl, and his brother, Charles.*

above: *The Good Bears of the World logo represents a charity that harnesses the comforting power of the teddy.*

the moon as it does in New York, Greece, Hollywood and Nether Wallop, i.e. that the moment I unpack and put Theodore on my bedside table with his friends and props, the strange place becomes a sort of home. I think he is a symbol of unloneliness. He sits there on his haunches (how he hates standing up!) reminding me of the happy and unhappy times we've had together, and his funny little face never fails to give me a little lift if things are looking a bit black.'

Throughout the 1960s and 1970s arctophiles became increasingly organized and sociable. In 1962 Colonel 'Bob' Henderson, an Army officer who had seen service in World War II under Field Marshal Montgomery, became president of the Teddy Bear Club (an organization without a formal membership, central offices or funds), which was formed to give recognition and support to fellow arctophiles. Colonel Henderson was fascinated by how the teddy bear seemed, for many, to

meet a psychological need. He explained this phenomenon in the following extract:

'From early times the bear has commanded a special place in folklore, myth, fairy-tale and legend. It has been regarded as a representative of both divine and natural forces; and today, in the form of the Teddy Bear, it is grasped in physical compensation and clung to for security. The reason for this is that the bear functions as a powerful symbol that provides satisfaction for a widespread psychological need. Consequently, history, religion, philosophy and psychology are all involved in any proper explanation of the Teddy Bear.

During the first half of the Twentieth Century it was found that the subtle appeal of the Teddy Bear was so endearing and enduring that the Teddy has become the lasting symbol of childhood, and consequently outlived all other mascot animals. It is now realised that anybody who thinks the Teddy Bear is just a cuddly toy and nothing more is very much mistaken. There is far more to Teddy than meets the eye. For there is now ample evidence to show that the Teddy Bear gives solace and enjoyment to people of all ages and both sexes. So much so, in fact, that this takes it right out of classification as a soft toy.

The Teddy Bear plays a great part in the psychological development of many people of all ages all over the world. This is because he is a truly international figure that is non-religious and yet is universally recognised as a symbol of love and affection. He represents friendship. He functions as a leavening influence amid the trials and tribulations of life.'

In 1970 an organization called Good Bears of the World was founded in the USA, encouraging collectors to raise

money for teddy bears to be given to sick and disadvantaged children. The organization was formally launched on Good Bear Day in 1973, when founders, including the US broadcaster and journalist James T. Ownby celebrated in Bern, Switzerland. This was followed up on 27 May 1979 with The Great Teddy Bear Rally, when more than 15,000 people and over 2,000 bears congregated in Wiltshire, England, at Longleat, home of the sixth Marquess of Bath, to raise money and toys for the children's charity Dr Barnardo's.

The growing number of adult bear collectors, plus books on how to make the toys, prompted a number of specialist dollmakers, known as doll artists, to start producing teddy bears in the early 1970s that were often dressed in intricate costumes. The first such bear on record was produced in the USA by Beverly Port, a doll artist from Retsil, Washington State, in 1974, and was shown at the International Dollmakers' Convention in Reno, Nevada that year.

Bear artistry may have emerged on the West Coast of the USA, but the form soon spread across the country and then to Britain, Australia, and continental Europe, particularly Germany, France and the Netherlands. Although bear artists proved highly successful, their output was significantly limited by the

above: *Today, Good Bears of the World give specially made teddies to sick and disadvantaged children.*

fact that each bear they produced was supposed to be handmade, or at least hand-finished. Cost was also an issue, as such finely crafted works were, by their very nature, highly exclusive. Thousands of would-be collectors were unable to afford artist-made bears, and it was this market that was being targeted when, during the mid- to late 1970s, a number of teddy-bear manufacturers – among them Gund, House of Nisbet and the North American Bear Co. – began to produce traditional-looking limited-edition toys.

House of Nisbet began life in Weston-super-Mare, England, in 1953 as Peggy Nisbet Ltd, a home-based industry making portrait dolls for the collectors' market. In 1975 the company was acquired by Jack Wilson, a Canadian, who changed its name to House of Nisbet and introduced a range of teddy bears designed by Peggy Nisbet's daughter, Alison (later to become Jack Wilson's wife). In the following year the company moved to Dunster Park, near Bristol, and in 1979 they began a highly successful collaboration with Peter Bull to try to design the ultimate teddy bear for the end of the century.

opposite: A traditionally made British bear, 1970s, mohair with plastic eyes, possibly Chad Valley.

The North American Bear Co. was founded in New York in the mid-1970s by Barbara Isenberg, who specialized in making unique teddy bears of an extremely high quality. In 1978, as the craze for jogging swept the nation, she started work on Albert the Running Bear, who wore a sweatshirt and pants. In the next year the company launched the first of its landmark Very Important Bear Series – teddy bears dressed as historical or literary characters such as Amelia Bearhart, Bearb Ruth, Cyrano de Beargerac and Scarlett O'Beara.

During the 1960s and 1970s, the face of teddy-bear manufacturing was transformed. At the beginning of the period the vast majority of bears were produced for children. This market remained, with makers gradually designing teddies that were softer and more huggable than before – Gund, in the USA, was particularly good at this, with its technique of understuffing its toys so that they were very floppy. Generally children's bears from this period were smaller than their traditional predecessors; they were also often unjointed. The increasing number of safety regulations introduced in the 1960s and 1970s meant that most companies started favouring flame-resistant materials as well as lock-in eyes and noses that could not be removed by a child.

Many companies with headquarters in the West decided to move their production of soft toys to Southeast Asia, in order to match the prices of goods emerging from countries such as Japan, Korea and China. The result was a multitude of cheap, throwaway bears of all shapes and sizes that could be given to loved ones, both young and old, without breaking the bank. The one thing that united these teddies was that, being badly produced out of poor materials, they were not intended to last.

A strong counterforce, though, committed to quality and durability, was the emerging adult collectors' market, which grew in the 1970s from the work of pioneer bear artists and was encouraged by leading arctophiles such as Peter Bull and Colonel 'Bob' Henderson. Teddy-bear collecting stopped being an underground movement and joined the list of mainstream hobbies. With this new status, it quickly gained momentum, until it was poised to take the world by storm in the last decades of the twentieth century.

Media Bears

Since 1907, when the Thomas A. Edison Co. made *The Teddy Bears*, the first moving picture featuring teddy bears, film and television have had a love affair with these toys. During the second half of the twentieth century many teddies made the leap from book or comic strip to television. Among the most successful were Teddy Edward, a Chiltern bear who from 1965 travelled the world for the BBC's *Watch with Mother*; Michael Bond's Paddington, the marmalade-loving bear who made his television debut in 1975; the mischievous glove puppet Sooty, given his own television show in 1955; and Yogi Bear, whose cartoons were seen around the world. Last, but by no means least, was Winnie the Pooh, whose adventures were transformed into a series of feature-length cartoons by Walt Disney Studios from 1966.

❶ *When Disney's feature-length animation of Rudyard Kipling's* The Jungle Book *was released in 1967, the undoubted star of the film was Baloo, a laid back bear who encourages the man-cub Mowgli to 'fall apart in my backyard' in his timeless song 'The Bare Necessities'. Steiff produced soft toys based on characters in the film, including Shere Khan the tiger, King Louie the ape, Hathi the baby elephant and, of course, Baloo.*

❶

❷ *One of the first teddy bears on television was the glove puppet Sooty, who was discovered on a talent show in 1952 and three years later had his own slot,* The Sooty Show. *With his co-presenter, Harry Corbett, and friends Sweep and Soo, Sooty was a mainstay of British television for the next twenty years. Harry's death in 1975 might have meant the end of Sooty's career had not his son, Matthew Corbett, taken over. Recently, Sooty was bought by a merchant bank intent on increasing his audience, so fans can expect to see a lot more of the little puppet in the near future.*

❷

❸ *Many of the photographs of Teddy Edward – the little bear who explored the world with photographers Patrick and Mollie Matthews – were taken in highly exotic or extreme locations, which most children could only ever dream of visiting. Others, however, were taken closer to home and could easily be experienced by young fans of his BBC television programme. This photograph, called* A Winter's Drive, *shows Teddy Edward taking his friends for a ride in his orange jeep.*

❹ *In 1961 A.A. Milne's widow sold the film rights to* Winnie the Pooh *to Walt Disney, who proceeded to make a series of animated features based on the stories. To date, six cartoons have been completed:* Winnie the Pooh and the Honey Tree *(1966),* Winnie the Pooh and the Blustery Day *(1968),* Winnie the Pooh and Tigger Too! *(1974),* The Many Adventures of Winnie the Pooh *(1977),* Winnie the Pooh and a Day for Eeyore *(1983) and* The Tigger Movie *(2000). During his transformation to the silver screen Pooh has gained a short red T-shirt and become even stouter than the E.H. Shepard original.*

❺ *In 1975 Michael Bond's stories about Paddington Bear were adapted for television by FilmFair. In the award-winning animations, a three-dimensional puppet of Paddington dominated a set where the backgrounds and all the other characters – including Mr and Mrs Brown, their children, Jonathan and Judy, and even his great friend Mr Gruber – were in two dimensions. The first series of thirty episodes, each lasting five minutes, was narrated by Sir Michael Hordern and shown in seventy-five different countries around the world. It was followed in 1979 by a second series of twenty-six episodes. Nearly twenty years later the French animators Cinar produced a new series of films.*

chapter 6

THE BEAR AS COLLECTABLE

(1980–2002)

*above: R. Dakin &
Co., Mishka, 1980,
designed for the Games
of that year and seen
holding the five
Olympic rings.*

The last two decades of the twentieth century saw a remarkable turnaround in the fortunes of the bear. When an unjointed plush teddy called Mishka (designed by the Russian artist Viktor Chizhikov for the Californian manufacturer R. Dakin & Co.) was chosen as the official mascot of the 1980 Moscow Olympic Games, it was clear that the toy's popularity was once more in the ascendant, but nothing could have prepared manufacturers and collectors for the public's reaction to the dramatization (by UK station Granada TV) of Evelyn Waugh's novel *Brideshead Revisited*, first shown in 1981.

Although much of Waugh's novel, published in 1945, depicts an aristocratic family torn apart by religious differences, it is most famous for its evocation of a golden era at Oxford University between the wars, when lasting friendships were formed in an atmosphere of innocence that was never to be recaptured. In the following passage the narrator, Charles Ryder, describes his first glimpse of Sebastian (played in the Granada production by Anthony Andrews) and his teddy bear, Aloysius:

'My first sight of him was in the door of Germer's and on that occasion I was struck less by his looks than by the fact that he was carrying a large teddy bear.

"That", said the barber as I took his chair, "was Lord Sebastian Flyte. A *most* amusing young gentleman."

"Apparently," I said coldly.

"The Marquis of Marchmain's second boy ... What do you suppose Lord Sebastian wanted? A hair-brush for his teddy bear; it was to have very stiff bristles, *not*, Lord Sebastian said, to brush him with, but to threaten him with spanking when he was sulky. He bought a very nice one with an ivory back and he's having 'Aloysius' engraved on it – that's the bear's name."'

The teddy bear who played Aloysius in the television series was actually called Delicatessen and belonged to the actor, author and arctophile Peter Bull, who described him as follows:

'Born 1907 in Sacco, Maine, USA. Sat on the shelf of a Dry Goods and Grocery store for fifty-five years.

Presented to me in 1969 by the owner, Miss Euphemia Ladd, who thought her teddy needed a change and liked the look of my little lot on the Johnny Carson Show. On arrival in the Bull hug he was christened Delicatessen, not realizing that this was going to be changed by sensational events and deed poll in the seventies. When the television series of *Brideshead Revisited* was first mooted by Granada it had never crossed our minds that we had a potential world star on our hands. At the audition (there were four other actors up for the part) Delicatessen romped home. In the television film he scored a notable success. He even won an award from the magazine *Time Out* "for the best performance in most trying circumstances". This pleased him greatly. Delicatessen became Aloysius.'

Delicatessen did indeed become Aloysius on 21 February 1982, when his name was 'officially' changed by deed poll. After his performance there was a surge of interest in traditional-looking teddies; long-forgotten bears were taken down from the attic, while for those unfortunates who had never had a teddy, or who had lost their childhood friend, companies such as the North American Bear Co. and House of Nisbet were on hand to provide Aloysius lookalikes. In Hollywood Aloysius received the ultimate accolade – his pads were impressed in the cement outside Mann's Chinese Theater on Sunset Boulevard. After Bull's death in May 1984 most of his bears were given to the London Toy and Model Museum. A few were sold, however, including Aloysius, who now lives with Ian Pout at Teddy Bears of Witne, Oxfordshire.

REPLICA BEARS

The leading teddy manufacturers were quick to respond to the demand for traditional-looking bears. In Germany Steiff celebrated 100 years of producing the finest soft toys by issuing its first limited-edition teddy, Papa Bear, in 1980. Based on the company's earliest designs, Papa Bear was 43cm (17in) tall, jointed and made from golden

below: *American, Aloysius, 1907. The star of* **Brideshead Revisited** *is pictured in a Daks Simpson scarf, with the novel that made him famous.*

mohair plush, with excelsior stuffing and black glass eyes. Only 11,000 of these bears were produced, 5,000 destined for the English-speaking world. In 1991 the first true Steiff replica was made – a copy of the thread-jointed Bär 35 PB first seen in 1904. This was followed in 1993 by a reproduction of the 1905 disc-jointed Bär 35 PAB, known as Bärle. Both bears were meticulously cut from traditional high-quality mohair using the original pattern. They were then stuffed with excelsior, their noses and mouths were embroidered and their glass eyes attached. They met with an enthusiastic response from collectors, and are now valuable in their own right.

Since 1980 Steiff has continued to produce replicas of some of its most famous designs, including Alfonzo, Blue Bear, Black Bear, Teddy Clown, Teddy Rose, Dolly Bear, Teddy Dicky and Teddy Baby. It is important to note that, for the first time in its history, Steiff has been making soft toys aimed at the collector rather than the child – most of the replicas are far too valuable to be subjected to the demands of a loving toddler. The bears, which are issued in presentation boxes complete with numbered certificates, are designed to enable arctophiles around the world to complement their collections with landmark bears from the past, closing gaps that would otherwise be impossible to fill because of the rarity and cost of the originals.

In the same year that Steiff began to produce replica bears it opened a company museum at its headquarters in Giengen, where exhibits include some of the oldest soft toys in existence. On 1 April 1992 it formed the Steiff Club as a forum for Steiff lovers and collectors. Members receive copies of the company magazine and can attend regional club meetings to discuss new products, listen to lectures or exchange bears. They also have the opportunity to buy special limited-edition bears exclusive to members. By using such innovative marketing techniques, as well as maintaining its pursuit of excellence, Steiff has succeeded in remaining at the forefront of teddy-bear manufacture.

Two events that had a dramatic effect on the German teddy-bear industry in general were the collapse of the Berlin Wall in November 1989 and the subsequent reunification of East and West Germany on 3 October 1990. Families that had fled to the West were able to return to their homes for the first time in forty years, Communist-run businesses were handed back to the descendants of their former owners, and, significantly in this age of the replica teddy, many original patterns were unearthed in long-forgotten archives.

below: *The entrance to Margarete Steiff GmbH as it is today. A company museum shares the site with the factory.*

Gebrüder Hermann KG, which had relocated from East to West Germany between 1948 and 1953, made its first foray into the adult collectable world with the launch in 1984 of Model 63, a replica of the company's earliest teddy bear. The experiment was a success and other replicas followed, including in 1990 a limited-edition bear to celebrate the reunification of Germany – he had the colours of the German flag on the pad of his right foot and a matching bow around his neck. In the next year the company issued a replica of a bear first produced by Bernhard Hermann in Sonneberg in 1922. The year 2000 saw the relaunch of a bear first released in 1930, along with new teddies such as a 40cm (16in) fisherman, dressed in knitted sweater and tweed trousers and equipped with

fishing rod, bucket and net. All the company's bears carry around their necks a red seal that reads 'HERMANN Teddy ORIGINAL' in gold; since 1994 a miniature seal has also been attached to their necks. Today Hermann bears are considered to be good value for money, and the dressed bears are particularly prized.

above: Alfonzo (left), Princess Xenia of Russia's teddy bear, seen alongside his replica, also made by Steiff.

The new political situation in Germany allowed Max Hermann's granddaughter, Dr Ursula Hermann, to return to Sonneberg in the former Eastern bloc and examine the family archives. In 1990, using the information she uncovered, Hermann-Spielwaren GmbH issued its Jubilee Bear – a replica of Max Hermann's 111 Series first released in the 1920s – to celebrate the company's seventieth anniversary. In 1991 two more early Max Hermann teddies were reproduced as limited editions of 3,000: the award-winning Bear 115 and Bear 113, which first appeared in a Sonneberg catalogue of 1929.

Among the firms returned to private ownership after the reunification of Germany was another Sonneberg toy company, H. Josef Leven, which had been run by the Communists since 1945. In 1990 Leven was handed back to Dora-Margot Hermann, the daughter of one of the joint owners, who had married Max Hermann's son Rolf-Gerhard in 1951. Hermann-Spielwaren now controlled Leven, and in 1992 it issued a limited-edition replica of a 1910 Leven bear to mark the event. (Similarly, in 1992, the Czech firm Hamiro collaborated with H. Scharrer & Koch GmbH, known as Sigikid, to produce replica teddy bears at their new Miro factory in Rokycany.) On 8 May 1999 Hermann-Spielwaren celebrated the centenary of the birth of its founder with the Max Hermann Classic Birthday Bear.

In Britain Peter Bull's collaboration with House of Nisbet, which had begun in 1979, bore fruit with the launch of the Bully Bear range of teddies and books in 1981. The bears, with their triangular heads, had an American look about them, which was hardly surprising as they were based in part on Peter Bull's Delicatessen, a US citizen. The company worked with Peter Bull again in 1984, when it produced a limited edition of his twelve bear books, *The Zodiac Bears*, accompanied by soft-toy versions of the series' characters. In 1987 House of Nisbet's owner, Jack Wilson, invented a method for distressing mohair using a turn-of-the-century velvet-crushing machine. The process was used to produce the company's version of Delicatessen, capitalizing on the success of *Brideshead Revisited*.

In 1989 House of Nisbet was bought by the US company Dakin Inc., which in turn was taken over by Applause in 1995. Wallace Berrie had bought the Applause Co. from Knickerbocker Toys in 1984, after his success during the 1970s in merchandising the Smurfs. (These cartoon characters first appeared in Belgium in *Le Journal de Spirou* on 23 October 1958. Drawn by Pierre Culliford, who was better known as Peyo, the Smurfs were three apples tall, had blue skin and wore white trousers and caps.) Applause became the new company name, and a series of licensing deals during the 1980s and 1990s (including Disney©, Sesame Street™ and Raggedy Ann™) ensured that it began the twenty-first century as a highly successful toy multinational. Since 1995 the company's output has been divided into two areas: Applause™, which concentrates on children's toys, such as Pokémon™ merchandise, and Dakin™ which produces high-quality plush gifts, including teddy bears, for adult collectors.

In this period, the two oldest surviving British teddy-bear manufacturers, Merrythought and Dean's, also entered the collectors' market. In 1986 Merrythought introduced a replica of its Magnet Bear, which had appeared in its first catalogue in 1930. This was followed in 1992 by limited-edition copies of Donald Campbell's Mr Whoppit, complete with embroidered bluebird badge, and Bingie, one of their most successful lines of the 1930s. In the autumn of 1995 Merrythought founded its own collectors' club and the following year introduced a replica Farnell bear, a fitting tribute to a company that had led the way in British teddy-bear design.

Dean's, in Pontypool, South Wales, produced some limited-edition bears in the early 1980s specifically for the US market, but it was not until 1991, three years after

left: *Leylani. This beautifully made and highly romantic teddy is by the award-winning Dutch bear artist Audie Sison.*

We are going to Pam Hebbs Teddy Bear Shop

Neil and Barbara Miller bought the company, that the production of collector bears began to overtake toymaking. Dean's is now a family business once again, with the Millers designing the range (with the exception of their artist-designed bears) and producing the company's catalogues, brochures and Internet site themselves. They are currently developing a museum of Dean's products, buying back important pieces at auction whenever they can.

above: A string of miniature bears by Elizabeth Leggat advertise Pam Hebbs' famous London shop.

One of the great success stories of the last decades of the twentieth century was Canterbury Bears Inc., which was established in 1980 by John Blackburn (a member of the Society of Industrial Artists and Designers) and his daughter Kerstin after a commission for a traditional-style jointed bear the previous year. The business flourished, and soon John's wife, Maude, and his other children, Mark and Victoria, also became involved. The firm produced a classic range of bears, limited editions and replicas, as well as fulfilling one-off commissions. During the late 1980s it produced a series of exclusive bears for institutions such as Liberty, Harrods and the Victoria & Albert Museum. In the early 1990s the US toy manufacturer Gund had exclusive distribution rights for Canterbury Bears in Canada and the USA.

BEAR ARTISTS

The number of artists around the world producing handmade bears continued to increase during the last two decades of the twentieth century. Their output was naturally much smaller than that of the larger manufacturers producing teddies for the collectors' market, but their work remained highly influential and was encouraged by the introduction of the Golden Teddy awards in 1987, followed by the TOBY (or Teddy Bear of the Year) awards in 1990.

Traditional-style teddy bears, both dressed and undressed, have remained favourites of artists and collectors alike. Among the best exponents to emerge in this field in recent years is Audie Sison, a Dutchman who started collecting artists' bears in 1990 and began producing his own designs, under the trademark A Teddy … by Audie, five years later. Since then he has won numerous prizes, including two TOBYs, a Golden Teddy and the prestigious Golden Teddy 'Winners' Circle'.

Gregory Gyllenship's traditional bears owe a great debt to early Steiff teddies, with their long arms that allow the toy to stand on all fours. Made out of the finest mohair plush, and with boot-button eyes, they are a fitting tribute to the great days of bearmaking. The London-based artist also produces large soft huggable bears, including polar bears, with realistic pads on their paws.

Wherever possible Sandra Wickenden of Wickenden Bears uses traditional materials such as excelsior stuffing, top-quality mohair plush, wool felts, hardboard joints and old boot-button eyes for her bears. Many of her creations are undressed, although some wear old collars, laces or leather muzzles sourced from antiques markets. She also produces realistic multijointed bears, sculpting their noses, mouths and claws in great detail from leather so that they look like the wild animals.

Janet Clark started making bears in 1991, selling them at local craft fairs. Since then this award-winning artist has moved on to produce limited-edition bears and other animals under the business name Teddystyle. She specializes in producing realistic toy bears, including American Black, Chi (a panda) and Kermode (a polar bear), as well as beautifully accessorized dressed bears, such as an organ-grinder complete with monkey. Since 1994 Janet has designed for Dean's Artist Showcase.

Scottish bear artist Elizabeth Leggat began designing and making traditional teddies in 1995. From the beginning she has produced miniatures, having been inspired by a tiny Schuco bear many years earlier. Using an ageing technique developed through trial and error, she gives her bears the gently faded and worn look of genuinely old teddies. The shapes of the bears, with their pronounced snouts, long arms, large feet and humped backs, are also reminiscent of early designs. Elizabeth

left: *One of British bear artist Gregory Gyllenship's highly huggable teddies.*

above: *Steiff, Teddy
Girl, 1904. Colonel
'Bob' Henderson's
remarkable bear.*

1990, is famous for her one-off designs, characterized by cartoonlike faces with large close-set eyes and smiling eyes. Each bear is carefully accessorized to create the distinctive character that has become her trademark and gained her recognition with collectors around the world. Jo Greeno has also designed bears for Dean's Artist Showcase.

BEARS UNDER THE HAMMER

Replica and artist-made bears have been hugely successful, but for those with the means there is no substitute for owning an original. Since the early 1970s Christie's and Sotheby's have included old and rare antique teddy bears in their collectors' sales, but at first they often appeared with no more than a simple one-line description. It was not until the early 1980s that sales of bears took off, and prices have been rising exponentially since, as a dwindling pool of good-quality bears is sought by a growing number of collectors. Bears from many different manufacturers are now extremely valuable, with the most expensive being early Steiff bears, particularly those with an interesting provenance. A blond Steiff dating from 1905 sold at Sotheby's in May 1985 for £2,090. Previously no bear had made more than £1,000. This was followed in February 1987 by a new world record of £5,720, paid at Sotheby's for a large yellow plush Steiff teddy of around 1904 named Archibald. In May 1987 £8,800 was paid, again at Sotheby's, by a US collector for a rare white muzzled Steiff bear of 1913. A similar but smaller bear sold in the same sale for £6,050. Then in May 1989, Christie's sold Alfonzo, the red plush Steiff

Leggat takes equal care when dressing her bears: she scours antiques fairs for a variety of old fabrics, trimmings and accessories to use in their costumes, Edwardian hand-embroidered cottons, silks and laces being special favourites, embellished with tiny old buttons and velvet flowers.

Not all artists specialize in producing traditional-looking teddies, however. Jo Greeno, who worked as a headteacher before becoming a professional bearmaker in

who had belonged to Princess Xenia, the second cousin of Tsar Nicholas II of Russia, for £12,100, then an enormous sum to pay for a teddy bear. He now takes pride of place in Ian Pout's collection at Teddy Bears of Witney, Oxfordshire.

A few months later, Alfonzo's crown was stolen by Happy, a 1926 dual plush Steiff with unusually large and seductive brown eyes. It was these eyes that captured the hearts of Paul and Rosemary Volpp, who paid £55,000 for her at Sotheby's on 19 September 1989, gaining her a place in *The Guinness Book of Records* as the most expensive bear in the world. Since then Happy and the

Volpps have travelled the globe together, raising large sums of money for charity. In 1990 Steiff introduced a limited-edition replica of Happy so that other collectors could share in the beauty of this extraordinary bear.

Steiff's black bears have consistently commanded top prices in recent years, which is ironic considering the poor reception that met the first sample in 1907. The limited numbers – a total of 494 bears were produced in 1912 in response to the *Titanic* tragedy – have certainly helped to fan collector interest. At Sotheby's in May 1990 a black Steiff called Othello was sold to Ian Pout for

below: *The auction of Teddy Girl at Christie's on 5 December 1994.*

right: *Steiff, Happy, 1926.*
The first teddy to appear in the
Guinness Book of Records *as*
the most expensive bear
in the world.

£24,200. The 48cm (19in) bear had a black stitched snout with a central seam, black boot-button eyes on red felt discs, a hump back and swivel joints, was stuffed with excelsior and was complete with growler. In October of the same year another 1912 black Steiff was auctioned at Phillips for £8,800 after being bought fifteen years previously from an antique shop for £14. As an indication of the price rises for black bears during the last decade of the twentieth century, on 4 December 2000 a black Steiff was sold by Christie's for £91,750.

On 6 December 1993 around 800 collectors and enthusiasts crowded into Christie's South Kensington for the first ever auction devoted exclusively to teddy bears (previously they had merely been sold alongside dolls and other toys). The highlight was Elliot, the unique blue bear that had failed to convince the Harrods store buyer as a sample in 1908. His rarity meant that there was no shortage of bidders this time round, and he eventually sold to a Canadian private collector for £49,500. Steiff produced an exclusive replica of Elliot for its club members in 1994–5.

Auctioneers and antique dealers may for some time have been aware of the increasingly large prices being paid for teddy bears, but it was the sale of Teddy Girl on 5 December 1994 that brought the phenomenon to the world's attention. In front of more than 500 collectors packed into two salerooms at Christie's South Kensington she broke all existing records when she sold for a staggering £110,000. Teddy Girl had been the lifelong companion of the late Colonel 'Bob' Henderson. After serving in World War II (with Teddy Girl at his side), Colonel Henderson devoted his life to collecting bears of all shapes and sizes, becoming one of the world's most respected arctophiles.

Teddy Girl was famous in her own right: she appeared at numerous conventions and featured in many publications as part of her work for Good Bears of the World, the organization dedicated to providing teddy bears for sick and disadvantaged children. This richly documented provenance was doubtless responsible for her achieving such a remarkable

above: *The IZU Teddy Bear Museum in Japan. Teddy Girl's new home, where she continues to comfort children in need.*

price, but as a 1904 cinnamon Steiff with a rare centre seam she was always going to be coveted by collectors.

Teddy Girl was purchased by Yoshihiro Sekiguchi, president of the Japanese toy company Sun Arrow. He outlined his plans for the next stage in her career soon after the auction: 'Teddy Girl is the most special bear in

the world, and I will ensure she is the centrepiece of my new museum. I intend to carry on in the footsteps of Colonel 'Bob' who used Teddy Girl to help children in need, and I will use her to help them in Japan.'

Collectors are extremely protective of their bears and hate to hear of them being mistreated. In May 1996 the well-known paranormalist Uri Geller paid £11,500 for a 122cm (4ft) bear that dated from the 1920s. During World War II soldiers in Vienna had used this teddy for bayonet practice until he was rescued by a compassionate Russian officer and given to two-year-old Gerhild Radakovic. Over fifty years later, Radakovic decided to sell him and donate part of the proceeds to an orphanage in Bosnia.

In the opening years of the twenty-first century the demand for teddy bears shows no sign of abating. At the Giengen Steiff Festival in 2000 the oldest known bear in the world was sold for £82,000. Dating from 1904, the extremely rare Bär 28 PB was in remarkable condition – indeed, his fragile sealing-wax nose was still intact. At the same festival a Margarete Steiff elephant pincushion, dating from 1893, was sold for a very modest £15,000. Although it was necessary to put prices on these two pieces at auction, their historical value is immeasurable.

Remarkably, at the time of writing it is a modern bear that holds the world record. On 14 October 2000 a limited edition of forty Steiff bears was offered at Teddies de l'an 2000, an auction whose proceeds were dedicated to the humanitarian organization Monaco Aide et Présence (MAP), which has

HSH Crown Prince Albert of Monaco as its honorary president. Each lot had been accessorized by a famous fashion house, Louis Vuitton, notably, customizing U Pitchoun (The Little One). This 45cm (18in) bear had jointed arms, legs and head, and was made of the finest mohair stuffed with woodshavings. His haute-couture outfit, which included a mackintosh, sou'wester, trousers, poloneck jumper and luggage, helped him to secure the astonishing price of £130,000. Although it was a charitable event – with Christie's staff donating their services at the auction – and for that reason does not perhaps accurately reflect the state of the bear market, this was a world record nonetheless.

opposite: *The young 'Bob' Henderson, pictured with his mother and Teddy Girl. The bear remained with Colonel Henderson throughout his life.*

below: Steiff and Louis Vuitton, U Pitchoun, 2000. This beautifully accessorized bear was sold for £130,000 in October 2000.

U Pitchoun's buyer, Mr Jessie Kim, owns a group of Korean toy companies. An admirer of both Steiff and Louis Vuitton, he is keen to promote widespread interest in collecting teddy bears in his homeland, where the pastime is virtually unknown. He opened a museum on Chesu Island in South Korea in March 2001, in which pride of place is given to the Louis Vuitton Steiff.

One unfortunate consequence of the record-breaking prices now paid for some bears has been the emergence in recent years of fake teddies, particularly ones purporting to be made by Steiff. When examining a bear alleged to be old, check that the materials used are correct for the period (mohair plush, felt pawpads, boot-button eyes for an early Steiff), that wear and tear has occurred in likely places (such as around the ears), and that any identifying buttons or labels are consistent with the period. If in doubt, check with an expert before parting with any money.

below: Teddy Bear Times, *which was launched in 1990, is just one of many modern magazines for arctophiles.*

THOUGHTS TO BEAR IN MIND

Since the 1980s hundreds of thousands of words have been written about the teddy bear in books and magazines. Shops devoted to the toys are now a common sight on the high street, while in 1986 the first museum exclusively dedicated to the teddy bear opened in Berlin and was swiftly followed by similar centres around the world. The Golden Teddy and TOBY awards promote excellence in bear design, while numerous clubs, conventions and shows ensure that the passion felt by collectors, manufacturers and bear artists is never spent. In recent years the Internet, with its websites, chat rooms and notice boards, has enriched the field of arctophily beyond the imaginings of previous generations.

Today, according to *American Heritage* magazine, the average US child aged two or older spends fours hours a day, about a quarter of his or her waking life, watching television. By the time they are eighteen, US children have been exposed to no fewer than 350,000 commercials. It would seem that manufacturers will go to any lengths to promote the latest plastic toys – through television, film and video games – and yet the teddy bear refuses to be ousted from our hearts.

A teddy is completely different from any other toy, and buying a bear has often more to do with falling in love than acquiring a status symbol. This recognition of

the One and Only was beautifully described by Christopher Milne, the proud owner of the original Pooh, in *The Enchanted Places*: 'A row of teddy bears sitting in a toyshop, all one size, all one price. Yet how different each is from the next. Some look gay, some look sad. Some look standoffish, some look lovable. And one in particular, that one over there, has a specially endearing expression. Yes, that is the one we would like, please.'

Most children still have at least one teddy bear of their own. Some are proudly on show; others wait patiently in the toy cupboard for the day when their owners need a hug or some reassurance. Their loyalty is often rewarded – teddy bears are the toys least likely to be thrown or given away. Some bears will be forgotten, but others will encourage their young owners to join the ever-increasing number of collectors around the world.

During the first century of the teddy bear, the toy went from being in enormous demand to facing near-extinction, before rising from the ashes to find new markets. Who knows what the next century will bring? One thing is for certain: this most resilient of toys will still be around bringing joy and comfort to millions.

above: *More and more fakes are being made today. The bear on the left is a genuine Steiff; on the right is a fake.*

Celebrity Bears

Modern bears dressed by celebrities from the worlds of fashion, music and television are commanding some of the highest prices at auction today. In 2000 Steiff produced a limited edition of eighteen bears. Each one was customized by a celebrity and offered for auction on 28 November at Home House, London, in aid of the Red Cross. Highlights included Sebastian Bear, dressed by the actor Anthony Andrews as a witty reference to his famous role in *Brideshead Revisited*; a stetson-wearing bear by Madonna, which reflected the singer's image on her *Music* album, released in 2000; and an aviator bear by high-flying entrepreneur Richard Branson.

❶ *Dressed in a Chinese silk red dress with matching undergarments, and carrying a miniature violin, this musical bear was designed by the virtuoso Vanessa-Mae. The glamorous violinist, who was born in 1979, was given her first piano lesson at the age of three. Two years later she took up the violin. In 1989 she gave her debut orchestral concert, and the following year she released her first album, Violin. Today, she is known for her wide repertoire, which includes pop music played on an electric violin.*

❷ *This exquisite bear was inspired by the court of the King of Siam from the Rodgers and Hammerstein musical* The King and I, *which opened at the London Palladium in 2000. The production starred Elaine Paige, the queen of British musical theatre, as Anna. Other highlights from Elaine's career include* Evita *(1978),* Cats *(1981),* Chess *(1986) and* Piaf *(1993). In 1996 she made her Broadway debut playing Norma Desmond in the stage adaptation of* Sunset Boulevard.

❸ *Wearing a scarlet tutu with matching ballet shoes, this dancing bear was created by Darcey Bussell, principal ballerina with the Royal Ballet. Darcey started ballet lessons aged thirteen, which is considered relatively late, but quickly caught up with and surpassed her contemporaries, winning the Prix de Lausanne in 1986. After a brief time at Sadlers Wells, she became a soloist for the Royal Ballet – the youngest ever dancer to hold this position.*

④ *With its heavenly wings and devil's horns, Devilish Angel is a clever combination of innocence and mischief. This bear was dressed by fifteen-year-old singing sensation Charlotte Church, who was born in Llandaff, Cardiff. From an early age Charlotte was drawn to perform, taking the stage at every opportunity. She was 'discovered' when she responded to an appeal on the British television show* This Morning *with* Richard and Judy. *Further television appearances led to a series of high-profile concerts and three albums, including* Voice of an Angel.

⑤ *Elvis Bear, dressed in black leather jacket, trousers and boots, pays homage to the king of rock 'n' roll. The teddy was designed by Holly Johnson, the former lead singer of Frankie Goes to Hollywood. Holly was born in Liverpool in 1960. From an early age he worked as a multimedia artist, inspired by the work of Andy Warhol, and combined silkscreen printing with band membership. In 1983 he was due to go to art college when Frankie Goes to Hollywood was signed. Their song 'Relax' sold millions of records when it was released the following year.*

THE BEAR NECESSITIES

The following section aims to provide information for established arctophiles and would-be collectors. Collectors' tips offers guidelines to those thinking about starting a collection, and highlights some of the pitfalls that can trip up even the most experienced buyers. The glossary explains the more technical terms used in this book and is followed by a list of the most important museums, manufacturers and bear artists in the world today. Finally, the bibliography suggests further reading for those wishing to continue their study of the teddy bear.

COLLECTORS' TIPS

Collecting teddy bears is a highly personal occupation. Like other collecting areas, arctophily is influenced by availability, funds and even market trends, but generally collectors are more interested in the bears' characters and histories than their material value. Full of character and charm, teddy bears provide a link with childhood and, perhaps, simpler times. They are fabulous companions and each and every one has its own distinct personality, especially the 'old boys' whose characters have undoubtedly been developed by the life they have led. One thing is certain, having made the decision to collect teddy bears, few are able to give up their new found friends.

MANUFACTURER

Choosing to collect one particular make of teddy bear is a highly personal affair. While one collector's passion may be Steiff and another's Chiltern, generally someone who collects teddy bears loves them all, whatever their shape, size, age or pedigree. The manufacturer does, however, play an important part when valuing a teddy bear. Steiff dominate the teddy bear market and are regularly responsible for the highest prices achieved at auction – indeed, the top ten prices for teddy bears are all held by Steiff. Other contemporary German manufacturers, such as Bing, Schuco and Jopi, are also highly sought after and good examples achieve strong prices at auction. Farnell are perhaps the leaders among British-made bears, but Merrythought, Chad Valley, Dean's and Chiltern are steadily increasing in both value and demand.

When buying, bear in mind that a teddy of known manufacture will almost always attract higher bids than one of unknown origin, however adorable.

MANUFACTURERS' TRADEMARKS

The most desirable teddy bears by a known manufacturer have their identifying labels, buttons or swing tags intact. Such completeness is rare, however, as many such trademarks have been either intentionally removed or lost through natural wear and tear. For example, since 1904 all Steiff bears have left the factory with a metal button in their left ear. Many parents removed the stud, which they thought might choke their small children. Others were removed by the children themselves, who were concerned that the buttons might be pinching the bears' ears and causing them some discomfort. While Steiff bears can be clearly identified without the aid of a button, their value can be affected by the absence of one. This applies to most, if not all, manufactured bears. In general, teddy bears that are in very good condition are likely to have their labels intact, whereas 'well-loved' examples are unlikely to have held on to any form of identification.

CONDITION

The condition of a teddy bear is very important and affects its value considerably. The vast majority of bears were played with by children, as was intended, and so show varying signs of wear and tear. The few bears that have remained in mint condition command the highest prices. Most injuries to a bear can be repaired, although some areas are more difficult to make good than others – and are more damaging to the toy's financial value. A bear's face, for example, is in many ways his fortune. A snout can be a vulnerable feature and a difficult area to repair discreetly. Loss of mohair to the body, on the other hand, can be concealed with the appropriate clothing. The eyes, paw pads and nose embroidery are further weakspots and a teddy bear discovered with all these features intact will certainly be more attractive to collectors than one that has undergone restoration. If, however, your chosen piece is restored, examine the merits of the work carried out. Be satisfied that it has been done sympathetically and in keeping with the bear's date and style of manufacture. Replaced eyes should be similar in design to those that have been lost; pads should be recovered in the same material as the originals; and re-embroidered noses should replicate the stitching used by the teddy's maker during its period of manufacture.

PERIOD OF PRODUCTION

While teddy bears spanning the entire period of production, from the earliest to the very latest, are collected, the date of manufacture undoubtedly has an effect on value. Early examples are of enormous historic interest and keenly sought after by collectors. It is therefore important to appreciate that the first teddy bears produced by any manufacturer will usually command a higher price than their later models.

RARITY

Bears that were unsuccessful when first launched, and so produced in limited numbers, are often now in demand because of their very rarity. Gebrüder Süssenguth's Peter bear, for example, was considered too frightening for children when it was launched in 1925, and few were sold. Today, the bear is highly prized by collectors. Prototype and sample bears are also extremely rare, as are special commissions and one-offs.

COLOUR

The vast majority of teddy bears produced were made using realistic natural-coloured mohair, such as blond and golden or pale brown. Any colour, therefore, regarded as out of the ordinary will attract collectors. Dark chocolate brown, cinnamon and apricot teddy bears are all quite unusual. Black is rare, as are the more outrageous colours, such as red, blue, green, purple and orange. Two-tone or dual plush mohair is also a rarity and therefore keenly looked for.

SIZE

Miniature teddy bears can be more easily displayed than their larger relatives and this can be a consideration for those collectors who are short of space. Desirability feeds demand, and smaller bears are often, inch for inch, more expensive than bigger models. Miniature bears with exceptional provenances, such as Peter Bull's Theodore or the Campbell twins' collection of Farnell soldier bears, will command high prices, but generally the top end of the market is dominated by larger bears.

PROVENANCE

Teddy bears are often seen as historical evidence of past childhoods. Any documentation, therefore, that accompanies a bear and illustrates its life is informative and valuable to collectors. Few bears are purchased directly from their original families, but when such a circumstance arises there is always the possibility of uncovering early photographs depicting the teddy and its owner, which can be tantalizing. If, however, a bear is offered with history unknown, the likelihood of tracing any documentation is slight, at best.

While documented provenance adds value to a bear, be certain that the material is in fact genuine. A 'story' without proof is not sufficient. If mentioned, the bear's history, however romantic, must be supported by relevant evidence often found in the form of photographs.

APPEAL

How a bear is perceived – its overall appeal – varies enormously from collector to collector. It is a well known fact that if two people fall in love with the same face, auction estimates may be ignored. While it is impossible to value the appeal of a bear, a handsome example wins over 'interesting' every time.

AUTHENTICITY

Fakes abound in any collecting area where items achieve significant prices at auction and the field of teddy bears is no exception to this rule. Since the 1980s, when early bears began to fetch five-figure sums, fake Steiffs and other sought-after toys have been found on the market, and as the prices for the best teddies have escalated so have the number of imitations.

If you have any doubts concerning the authenticity of a teddy bear try to seek the opinion of an expert – Christie's and the other leading auction houses offer free advice on pieces brought into their premises. It is worth considering that the majority of fakes in circulation have been bought at markets, car-boot sales and uncatalogued auctions, where collectors have had to make up their minds quickly and in a pressured environment. To avoid making an expensive mistake at such a venue read as much about the subject as possible beforehand, visit auction houses and museums and try to handle the genuine article. When buying an unautheticated teddy bear examine it carefully – taking into account the materials used and any specific design characteristics – and obtain a written receipt describing the toy (if the seller is unwilling to give this, walk away).

GLOSSARY

Airbrush – To spray paint over the plush using compressed air.

Alpaca plush – Plush made from the very soft wool of a South American mammal related to the llama.

Artificial-silk plush – Plush made from reconstituted wood pulp or other form of cellulose; used to imitate mohair plush.

Artist bear – A bear designed by an individual and finished by hand.

Boot-button eyes – Rounds made from compressed wood pulp with metal loops on back; conceived as shoe fasteners, they were adopted by the toy industry to be used as eyes.

Cotter pin – A split pin used to secure disc joints together.

Cotton plush – Plush made from cotton; an inexpensive alternative to mohair plush popular during and immediately after World War II.

Disc joints – Wooden or cardboard discs placed between the limbs and torso and fixed by a cotter pin; disc joints allow smooth and full movement of the limbs.

Dual plush – Coloured plush that is tipped with a second, contrasting colour.

Eccentric wheels – Wheels with a non-central axle that turn unevenly; toys with eccentric wheels seem to waddle or lumber.

Excelsior – See wood wool.

Felt – Soft fabric formed from matted wool fibres that have been worked together using steam, heat and pressure.

Googly eyes – Large, round plastic or glass eyes with pupils that move.

Growler – Internal voice box that produces a growl when the toy is tilted.

Hug – The collective noun for teddy bears.

Hump – The rounded protuberance across the shoulders of certain bears, particularly the grizzly.

Jointed bear – A bear with fully moveable head, arms and legs.

Kapok – Very light, soft fibre from tropical tree used for stuffing soft toys during the 1920s and 1930s.

Mohair – Long, soft silky hair of the Angora goat.

Mohair plush – Plush made from mohair blended with sheeps' wool or cotton.

Plush – Fabric with long, open pile that is softer than velvet.

Pull-cord voice – Internal voice box activated by pull cord.

Rexine – A shiny leather oilskin seen post World War II.

Rod-jointing – An internal jointing system that uses a series of rods running through the body.

Sealing wax – The wax used to seal letters, used in early teddy bear manufacture for realistic moulding.

Squeaker – Internal voice box that emits a squeak when the toy is squeezed.

String joints – Early type of jointing system, where the limbs and the head are joined to the torso by string.

Voice box – Internal mechanical device used to produce a sound and activated by squeezing or tipping a toy or tugging its pull cord.

Wood wool – Long, thin wood shavings used for stuffing toys; also known as excelsior.

TEDDY BEAR MUSEUMS

Aunt Len's Doll & Toy Museum

6 Hamilton Terrace
New York NY 10031
USA

The Bear's Loft

Abbey Dore Court Gardens
Abbey Dore
Nr Hereford HR2 0AD
UK

The Bear Museum

38 Dragon Street
Petersfield
Hampshire GU31 4JJ
UK

Berni Brumm's Teddy Museum

Hauptstrasse 98
8751 Leidersbach
Germany

Bethnal Green Museum of Childhood

Cambridge Heath Road
London E2 9PA
UK

The Bournemouth Bears

Old Christchurch Lane
Bournemouth BH1 1NE
UK

The Carrousel Shop & Museum

505 West Broad Street
Chesaning MI 48616
USA

Children's Museum of Indianapolis

P.O. Box 3000
Indianapolis IN 46206
USA

The Cotswold Teddy Bear Museum

76 High Street
Broadway
Worcester WR12 7AJ
UK

Deutsches Puppen- und Barenmuseum

Sonnegasse 8
5401 St Goar
Germany

The Golden Cross

Wixford Road
Ardens Grafton
Nr Bidford-on-Avon
Warwickshire B50 4LG
UK

Ironbridge Toy Museum

The Square
Ironbridge
Shropshire TF8 7AQ
UK

Käthe Kruse Poppenmuseum

Binnenhaven 25
1781 BK Den Helder
The Netherlands

Lakeland Motor Museum

Holker Hall
Cark-in-Cartmel
Grange-over-Sands
Cumbria LA11 7PL
UK

The London Toy and Model Museum

21–23 Craven Hill
London W2 3EN
UK

Merritt's Museum of Childhood

Route 422
Douglassville PA 19518
USA

Merrythought Museum

The Wharfage
Ironbridge
Shropshire TF8 7NJ
UK

Midland Good Bears

40 Fairfax Road
Sutton Coldfield
West Midlands B75 7JX
UK

Musée du Jouet

Rue de l'Association
2400 Brussels
Belgium

The Museum of Childhood

15A Central Avenue
Bangor
Co. Down
UK

Museum of Childhood

42 High Street
Edinburgh EH1 1TG
UK

Museum of Childhood Memories

1 Castle Street
Beaumaris
Anglesey
Gwynedd LL58 8AP
UK

Pollock's Toy Museum

1 Scala Street
London W1P 1LT
UK

Puppenhausmuseum – Basel

Steinenvorstadt 1
CH-4051 Basel
Switzerland

Ribchester Museum of Childhood

Church Street
Ribchester
Lanchester PR3 3YE
UK

Theodore Roosevelt's Birthplace

28 East 20th Street
New York NY 10003
USA

Speelgoed Museum

Nekkersoel 21
2800 Mechelen
Belgium

Speelgoedmuseum

Sint Vincentiusstraat 86
4901 GL Oosterhout
The Netherlands

Spielzeugmuseum

Baselstrauss 34
CH-4125 Richen
Switzerland

Spielzeugmuseum

Bürgerspitalgasse 2
A-5020 Salzburg
Austria

Spielzeugmuseum in Alten

Rathaustrum
Sammlung Ivan Steiger
Marienplatz 15
8000 München 2
Germany

Margarete Steiff Museum

Alleenstrasse 2
Postfach 1560
D-7928 Giengen-Brenz
Germany

Margaret Woodbury Strong Museum

1 Mathatten Square
Rochester NY 14607
USA

Teddy Bear Castle Museum

431 Broad Street
Nevada City CA 95959
USA

Teddy Bear House

Antelope Walk
Dorchester
Dorset DT1 1BE
UK

The Teddy Bear Museum

19 Greenhill Street
Stratford-upon-Avon
Warwickshire CV37 6LF
UK

Teddy Bear Museum of Naples

2511 Pine Ridge Road
Naples FL 33942
USA

Teddy Bears of Witney

99 High Street
Witney
Oxfordshire OX8 6LY
UK

Teddymuseum Klingenberg

W. und R. Koenig
In der Altstadt 7
63911 Klingenberg/Main
Germany

Toy and Teddy Bear Museum

373 Clifton Drive North
St Annes
Lytham St Annes
Lancashire FY8 2PA
UK

The Toy Emporium

79 High Street
Bridgnorth
Shropshire WV16 4DS
UK

The Wareham Bears

Wilton House
The Estate Office
Wilton
Salisbury SP2 0BJ
UK

BEAR ARTISTS

Jo Greeno

2 Woodhill Court
Woodhill
Send
Woking
Surrey GU23 7JR
UK

Gregory Gyllenship

109 Bow Road
London E3 2AN
UK

Pam Howells

39 Frognall
Deeping St James
Peterborough
Cambridgeshire PE6 8RR
UK

Elizabeth Leggat

9 Jamieson Drive
East Kilbride
Glasgow
Lanarkshire G74 3EA
UK

Norbeary Bears

14 Claymere Avenue
Norden
Rochdale
Lancashire OL11 5BW
UK

Sue Quinn

Dormouse Designs
The Old Drapery
Quarriers Village
Bridge of Weir
Renfrewshire PA11 3SX
UK

Robin Rive

Countrylife New Zealand
19 Thomas Peacock Place
Auckland 1006
PO Box 14-391 Panmure
New Zealand

Sue Schoen

9 Radnor Drive
Tonteg
Mid-Glamorgan CF38 1LA
UK

Audie F. Sison

27 Papelaan
2252 ED Voorschoten
The Netherlands

Teddy Style (Janet Clark Originals)

61 Park Road
Boxmoor
Hemel Hempstead
Hertfordshire HP1 1JS
UK

Sandra Wickenden

Wickenden Bears
28 Merevale Road
Gloucester GL2 0QY
UK

TEDDY BEAR CLUBS

Beer Bericht/Berefanclub

Prinzengracht 1089
1017 JH Amsterdam
The Netherlands

Club Français de l'Ours

70 Rue du Docteur Sureau
93160 Noisy Le Grand
France

Dean's Collectors' Club

Pontnewynydd Industrial Estate
Pontypool
Gwent NP4 6YY
UK

The Followers of Rupert

31 Whiteley
Windsor
Berks SL4 5PJ
UK

Good Bears of the World (UK) Trust

c/o Audrey Duck
256 St Margaret's Road
Twickenham
Middlesex TW1 1PR
UK

Good Bears of the World (USA) Trust

c/o Mrs Terrie Stong
PO Box 13097
Toledo OH 43613
USA

Hugglets Teddy Bear Club

PO Box 290
Brighton
East Sussex BN2 1DR
UK

In Teddies We Trust

PO Box 297
Rosebery
NSW 2018
Australia

Merrythought International

Collectors' Club
Dale End
Ironbridge
Telford
Shropshire TF8 7NJ
UK

Paddington's Action Club

Vincent House
North Parade
Horsham
West Sussex RH12 2PN
UK

Robin Rive Collectors' Club

c/o Countrylife New Zealand
Box 3604
Brentwood
Essex CM14 4RY
UK

Steiff Club

Margarete Steiff GmbH
Alleenstrasse 2
D-89537 Giengen/Brenz
Germany

Steiff Club USA

31 East 28th Street
9th Floor
New York NY 10016
USA

Teddy's Patch

Le Club des Amis de l'Ours
34 Rue Lieu de Sante
76000 Routen
France

TEDDY BEAR MAGAZINES

BärReport

Teddybär-Magazin GmbH
Venloer Str. 686
50827 Köln
Germany

Bear Facts Review

PO Box 503
Moss Vale
NSW 2577
Australia

In Teddies We Trust

28 Regent Arcade
Adelaide SA 5000
Australia

Teddy Bear and Friends

Cowles Magazines Inc.
6405 Flank Drive
Harrisburg PA 17112
USA

Teddy Bear Club International

Maze Media Ltd
Castle House
97 High Street
Colchester
Essex CO1 1TH
UK

The Teddy Bear Review

PO Box 1239
Hanover
PA 17331
USA

Teddy Bear Scene

EMF Publishing
EMF House
5–7 Elm Park
Feming
West Sussex BN12 5RN
UK

Teddy Bear Times

Avalon Court
Star Road
Partridge Green
West Sussex RH13 8RY
UK

Teddy Bear Tymes

7 Whiteoak Drive
St Catharines
Ontario L2M 3B3
Canada

TeddyBär und seine Freunde

Verlag Marianne Cieslik
Theodor-Heuss Str. 185
D-52428 Jülich
Germany

TEDDY BEAR WEBSITES

www.bearworld.com
www.tbonnet.com
www.teddybearandfriends.com

www.teddybearmagazine.com
www.teddybears.com
www.teddybearsearch.com

www.teddybeartimes.com
www.teddy-bear-uk.com
www.teddy-world.com

CHRISTIE'S ADDRESSES

Amsterdam

Cornelis Schuytstraat 57
1071 JG Amsterdam
Tel: 31 (0) 20 57 55 255
Fax: 31 (0) 20 66 40 899

Athens

26 Philellinon Street
10558 Athens
Tel: 30 (0) 1 324 6900
Fax: 30 (0) 1 324 6925

Bangkok

Unit 138-139, 1st Floor
The Peninsula Plaza
153 Rajadamru Road
10330 Bangkok
Tel: 662 652 1097
Fax: 662 652 1098

Edinburgh

5 Wemyss Place
Edinburgh EH3 6DH
Tel: 44 (0) 131 225 4756
Fax: 44 (0) 131 225 1723

Geneva

8 Place de la Taconnerie
1204 Geneva
Tel: 41 (0) 22 319 17 66
Fax: 41 (0) 22 319 17 67

Hong Kong

2203-5 Alexandra House
16-20 Chater Road
Hong Kong Central
Tel: 852 2521 5396
Fax: 852 2845 2646

London

8 King Street
St James's
London SW1Y 6QT
Tel: 44 (0) 20 7839 9060
Fax: 44 (0) 20 7839 1611

London

85 Old Brompton Road
London SW7 3LD
Tel: 44 (0) 20 7581 7611
Fax: 44 (0) 20 7321 3321

Los Angeles

360 North Camden Drive
Beverly Hills
CA 90210
Tel: 1 310 385 2600
Fax: 1 310 385 9292

Melbourne

1 Darling Street
South Yarra, Melbourne
Victoria 3141
Tel: 61 (0) 3 9820 4311
Fax: 61 (0) 3 9820 4876

Milan

1 Piazza Santa Maria delle Grazie
20123 Milan
Tel: 39 02 467 0141
Fax: 39 02 467 1429

Monaco

Park Palace
98000 Monte Carlo
Tel: 377 97 97 11 00
Fax: 377 97 97 11 01

New York

20 Rockefeller Plaza
New York
NY 10020
Tel: 1 212 636 2000
Fax: 1 212 636 2399

New York

219 East 67th Street
New York
NY 10022
Tel: 1 212 606 0400
Fax: 1 212 737 6076

Rome

Palazzo Massimo Lancellotti
Piazza Navona 114
00186 Rome
Tel: 39 06 686 3333
Fax: 39 06 686 3334

Singapore

Unit 3, Parklane
Goodwood Park Hotel
22 Scotts Road
Singapore 228221
Tel: 65 235 3828
Fax: 65 235 8128

Taipei

13F, Suite 302, No. 207
Tun Hua South Road
Section 2
Taipei 106
Tel: 886 2 2736 3356
Fax: 886 2 2736 4856

Tel Aviv

4 Weizmann Street
Tel Aviv 64239
Tel: 972 (0) 3 695 0695
Fax: 972 (0) 3 695 2751

Zurich

Steinwiesplatz
8032 Zurich
Tel: 41 (0) 1 268 1010
Fax: 41 (0) 1 268 1011

SELECT BIBLIOGRAPHY

Axe, J., *The Magic of Merrythought*, Hobby House Press, Inc., Cumberland, Maryland 1986; 2nd edition Merrythought, Ironbridge 1998

Cieslik, J. and M. *Button in Ear: The Steiff Encyclopedia*, Marianne Cieslik Verlag, Julich, Germany 1989

Cockrill, Pauline, *The Teddy Bear Encyclopedia*, Dorling Kindersley Ltd, London 1993

Cockrill, Pauline, *The Ultimate Teddy Bear Book*, Dorling Kindersley Ltd, London 1991

Cook, Carolyn (compiler), *Best of Teddy Bear & Friends Magazine – The Ultimate Authority*, Hobby House Press, Inc., Cumberland, Maryland 1992

Fox Mandel, Margaret, *Teddy Bears & Steiff Animals*, Collector Books, Paducah, Kentucky 1994

Hebbs, Pam, *Collecting Teddy Bears*, Pincushion Press Collectibles Series, New Cavendish Books, London 1992

King, Constance Eileen, *The Century of the Teddy Bear*, Antique Collectors' Club, Woodbridge, Suffolk 1997

Leibe, Frankie, with Leyla Maniera and Daniel Agnew, *Miller's Soft Toys: A Collector's Guide,* Octopus Publishing Group Ltd, London 2000

Mullins, Linda, *Fourth Teddy Bear & Friends Price Guide*, Hobby House Press, Inc., Cumberland, Maryland 1993

Mullins, Linda, *Teddy Bears Past & Present, A Collector's Identification Guide*, Hobby House Press, Inc., Cumberland, Maryland 1986

Mullins, Linda, *Teddy Bears Past & Present, Vol. II,* Hobby House Press, Inc., 1991

Pearson, Sue and Dottie Ayers, *Teddy Bears: A Complete Guide to History, Collecting, and Care*, Macmillan Publishers Ltd, London 1995

Pfeiffer, Guther, *Steiff – Sortiment, 1947–1999*, Taunusstein, Germany 1999

Pistorious, R. and C., *Steiff, Sensational Teddy Bears, Animals and Dolls*, Hobby House Press, Inc., Cumberland, Maryland 1990

Schoonmaker, Patricia W., *A Collector's History of the Teddy Bear*, Hobby House Press, Inc., Cumberland, Maryland 1981

Smith, Carol, *Indentification & Price Guide – Winnie the Pooh Collectibles, II*, Hobby House Press, Inc., Cumberland, Maryland 1996

Waring, Philippa, *In Praise of Teddy Bears – Collector's Edition*, Souvenir Press Ltd, London 1997

INDEX

acknowledgements

ACKNOWLEDGEMENTS

AUTHOR'S ACKNOWLEDGEMENTS

The author would like to say special thanks to:

Margarete Steiff GmbH for their support and loan of unique material, especially Falk Thomas, Martin Frechen and Manuela Fustig.

Ian Pout and all at Teddy Bears of Witney.

Lesley and Peter Earthy and all the Donnington Bears.

Peter and Leanda Woodcock

Slaney Begley

Jane Dymond

Dee Hockenberry

Sandra Wickenden

Audie Sison

Gregory Gyllenship

Elizabeth Leggat

Teddy Bear Times

Pat Rush

Good Bears of the World

Jill and George Mooratoff

GAF Günther Pfeiffer GmbH, especially Günther Pfeiffer.

A personal thank you to:

Ian Munro

Pam Hebbs, a dear friend who inspired me.

Dr Maniera, my brilliant sister, for her encouragement and strength.

My Mum, for her undivided devotion.

Alexa, for her sparkle and imagination.

All at Park House Farm.

And last, but not least, William.

PICTURE CAPTIONS

p.2 American, Aloysius, 1907. The star of *Brideshead Revisited* (Granada Television), formerly known as Delicatessen.

p. 20 *(Chapter 1)* A Steiff Bär 28 PB, c.1904. This early Steiff bear is believed to be one of the oldest surviving bears in the world. He was the immediate successor of Bär 55 PB.

p. 30 *(Chapter 2)* A group of bears manufactured by Steiff, Gebrüder Bing and Chiltern Toys, from the 'boom year' of 1908.

p. 70 *(Chapter 3)* A group of bears by Steiff, J.K. Farnell and Chiltern Toys, the leading manufacturers of the 'Roaring Twenties'.

p. 116 *(Chapter 4)* Steiff, Schreyer & Co. (Schuco) and Merrythought Ltd made these bears in the 1950s.

p. 136 *(Chapter 5)* Merrythought Ltd, Cheeky, 1970s. Merrythought's classic design was produced in synthetic simulated mink and had plastic eyes.

Page 150 *(Chapter 6)* Merrythought Ltd, James, 1993. A limited edition of one by Merrythought's design director Jacqueline Revitt, dressed as James Christie, founder of the auction house, and made to celebrate the very first auction devoted entirely to teddy bears at Christie's South Kensington.

TEXT CREDITS

p. 10 *Summoned by Bells,* John Betjeman, John Murray (Publishers) Ltd

p. 77 *Winnie the Pooh,* first published 14 October 1926, text by A.A. Milne, © under the Berne convention, used with the permission of Egmont Children's Books Ltd

PICTURE CREDITS

p. 69 (3) Reg Speller 1940, Hulton Getty, **p. 73** Howard Coster, Bridgeman Art Library, **p. 115** (3) © Express Newspapers, (5) © Granada Television Ltd, **p. 148** (2) © Granada Television Ltd, (4) © Disney Enterprises, Inc., (5) The Copyrights Group Ltd